GOD,
ARE WE
THERE YET?

GOD, ARE WE THERE YET?

Learning to Trust God's Direction in Your Life

ROBERT STOFEL

LIFE JOURNEY
Bringing Home the Message for Life

An Imprint of Cook Communications Ministries
COLORADO SPRINGS, COLORADO • PARIS, ONTARIO
KINGSWAY COMMUNICATIONS, LTD., EASTBOURNE, ENGLAND

Life Journey® is an imprint of
Cook Communications Ministries, Colorado Springs, CO 80918
Cook Communications, Paris, Ontario
Kingsway Communications, Eastbourne, England

GOD, ARE WE THERE YET?

First Printing, 2004
Printed in United States of America
1 2 3 4 5 6 7 8 9 10 Printing/Year 08 07 06 05 04

Cover Design: True Blue Design/Sandy Flewelling
Cover Photo: © Corbis

Library of Congress Cataloging-in-Publication Data

Stofel, Robert, 1962-
  God, are we there yet? : finding strength for the journey / Robert
Stofel.
      p. cm.
Includes bibliographical references.
  ISBN 0-7814-4079-3 (pbk.)
  1. Christian life--Anecdotes. I. Title.
BV4501.3.S762 2004
248.8'6--dc22
                                        2003023229

THIS BOOK IS LOVINGLY DEDICATED
TO THE MEMORIES OF

PATTI WHITEHURST
AND
MIKE NELSON

"BARRICADE THE ROAD THAT GOES NOWHERE;
GRACE ME WITH YOUR CLEAR REVELATION.
I CHOOSE THE TRUE ROAD TO SOMEWHERE,
I POST YOUR ROAD SIGNS AT EVERY CURVE AND CORNER."
—PSALM 119:29–30 MSG

Contents

FOREWORD

Every century has its keen observers. Things of life that rapidly pass and the unchangeable characteristics of daily reality are expounded by writers as varied as Mark Twain and Erma Bombeck.

Robert Stofel, like his hero, Charles Haddon Spurgeon, is a member in good standing of this illustrious group. In the vein of Spurgeon, Stofel is not only a superb commentator on the daily scene, but is blessed with the God-given talent of applying relevant, practical treatment with great insight to the full spectrum of daily living from a perspective of eternity's values.

Few are better equipped to write about a heavenly approach to the things of life than Robert Stofel. Here is a man that God has molded in the furnaces of affliction and trial. If A. W. Tozer was correct when he said that God could not use a person greatly until he had hurt him deeply, Rob Stofel will be a mighty voice for our heavenly Father.

I met Rob Stofel shortly after he graduated from high school. His body still bore the effects of drug and alcohol abuse. His mother-in-law told me that when he started to date her daughter, it was a parent's worst nightmare coming true. Yet when he came to a saving faith in Jesus Christ, the transformation was miraculous; he was immediately freed from the slavery of substance abuse.

As a husband and father with two small daughters, Stofel formed a small but successful painting company. With the work ethic of a Puritan, he carried a full load of college courses at Middle Tennessee

State University. And his grades were good enough to win him acceptance into the master of divinity program at Gordon-Conwell Theological Seminary.

Stofel never forgets an incident of his childhood in rural Tennessee. He frequently entertains friends and associates by recalling stories and events of saints and sinners who have crossed his path in the journey we call life. Stofel has the unique ability to weave their experiences into lessons of hope that remind us of God's sovereignty and control of our destiny. He is a man who not only loves the Lord but has the God-given gift to take the mundane things of daily existence and develop them into great spiritual truths presented as wonderful stories of lives in progress.

These spiritual anecdotes will deeply affect every reader.

Today, Rob is seminary student, a fine pastor, and a superb preacher. His stories of life with their practical applications have made him a much-sought-after speaker. It is a cause for great rejoicing that believers everywhere can now enjoy his modern-day parables.

Roy Clarke
Ponte Vedra Beach, Florida

ACKNOWLEDGMENTS

Thank you, Terry Whalin, for your encouragement and determination in getting this book published, and to the rest of the crew at Cook Communications Ministries for their meticulous work.

Thanks to my wife, Jill, who lets me write about her in a zany-comical way. She's been with me since high school and without me during most of the writing of this book. Thanks for your love and understanding—you've made me a better man and father.

Thanks to Blair and Sloan, my daughters, who also allow me to write about them, and who sigh only every now and then when they wind up in a sermon illustration. Your unconditional love for people and the church that sometimes wounds is beyond any expectations I may have had of you.

Thanks to Mom and Nick for their love and encouragement, and for the grant from the No-Nicker Foundation that supplied reams of paper, ink, envelopes, and other financial support through the writing of this book.

Thanks to Hickory Hills Community Church. You've supported me with prayer and much love. My journey with you and the things I've learned from you will never be forgotten. I've never been loved by a church as I've been loved by you. It's an honor to shepherd you.

Thanks to Roy Clarke for your guidance and wisdom. You've loved me like a son, and in some small way, I hope you've felt that you have one.

Thanks to my friends Todd and Sheri Hutchison, who know all about me and love me anyway.

Thanks to Johnny and Denise Hayes for your friendship and loyalty. Thanks for the lunches. The fried green tomatoes at Jack's are the best!

Thanks to Sanford and Chris Whitehurst for your support and unconditional love.

Thanks to Dad and my brother, Kerry, who planted a love for the art of storytelling in my soul at an early age while we leaned on the counter of J.B. Cook's Auto Parts in Franklin, Tennessee, and who listened to those madcap characters who graced the door and took some time to give us all Southern oral history.

Thanks to my pastor, Bruce Coble, for all the counseling and for the ride to my first Bible study at the age of nineteen. I knew nothing and you taught me Christ's love.

Thanks to Jerry and Susan Stofel for your encouragement and hospitality in Orange Beach.

Thanks to Larry, Luann, Jared, and Stephanie Black for the time you provided us at your home, The Legacy. What a view!

Thanks to Joe and Diana Carver for your friendship, wisdom, and hospitality while I attended school in Charlotte.

Thanks to Dale Earnhardt Jr. You've taught us all how to win.

STOP SIGNS, RED LIGHTS, AND OTHER PLACES TO WAIT

Understanding Why God Makes Us Wait

THE YEAR JOE NAMATH took the Jets to the Super Bowl my dad announced he was taking us on a family vacation. He said, "What we need is a good road trip. We need adventure! We need to see Rock City! I want to stand on that mountain!"

It was a monumental announcement—the dawning of the age of travel for the Stofel family. We'd been to tractor pulls and Saturday-night dirt racetracks and county fairs and Southern Gospel singings and local wrestling matches. We were well-rounded connoisseurs of entertainment, but to see Rock City Gardens, with its glow-in-the-dark caves, strolling costumed characters, and coin-operated binoculars through which one could purportedly see seven states raised the entertainment bar. It meant traveling, and traveling was what my brother and I were really after. So we climbed into the green Ford Torino with a euphoria that made us punch each other.

When Dad got into the car, he lectured us about good behavior and not asking questions. We nodded like two angels, knowing it was all a lie. Then he pulled out onto the highway and the tires moaned out a sleepy ballad through an early morning world that was eating its Wheaties while the sun bathed it with a radiant, unabashed yawn that stretched across the horizon. And miles and miles later, when the sun descended in the western sky, we popped the hated questions, "Where are we? Are we there yet?"

We'd heard Dad's lecture, but when questions are going off in your mind like fabulous yellow Roman candles in the American night, you have no choice but to let one escape.

He gave us his turned-to-the-side look, where one eye followed the road and the other shot flares that marked dangerous territory.

"I was just wondering," I said.

"We'll get there when we get there," he said in a prosaic tone.

"I just wanted—"

"I told you, we'll get there when we get there."

But no matter how hard Dad tried to suppress these questions, they had a way of popping out and assailing the back of his head about every fifty miles.

Every little boy and pigtailed girl has asked these questions on a family trip. Even as adults we never really get away from them, only now we direct them toward God, making them questions of doubt. "God, are we there yet?"; "How much longer will I have to wait?"; "Why aren't my dreams being fulfilled?"

These questions reveal the level of frustration that has built up over the years, and as adults we've stopped believing in the joy of the destination. Too much has happened. Too many inexplicable defeats have occurred. We feel as though we're headed nowhere. Yet we wait. We hope for passionate joy to be rekindled, creating a holy hush that allows us to hear once again the unrestrained voice, "Come to me, all of you who are weary and carry heavy burdens, and I will give you rest" (Matthew 11:28). Rest is what we need. But we are here. Rest is over there. And we don't know how to bridge the gap.

THE JOURNEY THROUGH WAITING

Most everyone is waiting to arrive at some destination. We may desire a certain career, hope for a marriage proposal, long for a healthy body, or crave some other dream that hasn't come true. But something happens when we outgrow the backseat and become the driver in the front. Anxiety enters. Details and circumstances get jumbled. Then there's the terrible ticking of time between departure and arrival. But there's a "passionate patience" to be discovered—a time of rest for weary souls, "because we know how troubles can develop passionate patience in us, and how that patience in turn forges the tempered steel of virtue, keeping us alert for whatever God will do next" (Romans 5:3 MSG). There's more to come. This is our hope. This is our "passionate patience." But can we wait? That's the question.

THE EXODUS THAT ALMOST FAILED

When God led the Israelites out of Egypt, their newfound freedom was as exhilarating for them as a modern-day teenager with a new driver's license; yet that freedom had its woes. They realized they would be facing danger and formed a militia. Maybe a meeting was called as they lined the Egyptian streets the way they did in the movie *The Ten Commandments*.

I can hear it now: "Okay, men, gather round. Listen up. I don't know what we're facing out there, but I know the Philistines are between us and total freedom. You've heard the rumors of giants and thugs. We need an army."

So they assembled an army, but it was a *Little Rascals* troop, complete with pots for helmets and pans for shields and sticks for weapons. They were a motley bunch, beating their chests and high-fiving each other, never realizing they were inadequately armed for battle.

Then God took Moses aside and said, "If the people are faced with a battle, they might change their minds and return to Egypt" (Exodus 13:17). So God instructed Moses to lead them "along a route through the wilderness toward the Red Sea, and the Israelites left Egypt like a marching army" (Exodus 13:18). I love that imagery. We can picture them marching off to battle in the wrong direction! Matthew Henry says, "They marched like an army with banners, which added much to their strength and honor."[1]

The Philistines, who lived by the sword, would have defeated them, and what seemed to be a long wait—a long journey to the Promised Land—was God protecting them. But they never got it. The only thing they got was the way the menu changed. They wanted the same kinds of food they were used to in Egypt. In Egypt they were slaves, but they had choices—marinated meat or fish, and a choice of fruit.[2]

Now they were running lean in the desert, whining and complaining about the camp food. They never imagined manna being their sole food, and God seemed to be the God of a one-course meal. It was manna Pop-Tarts for breakfast, Big Manna sandwiches for lunch, topped off with a manna casserole for dinner. They were hungry for junk food when God was feeding them the dew of heaven. And maybe they huddled in their tents at night and designated a runner to go to the south side of Egypt to the late night drive-through at Wendy's. Who knows what they were doing, other than complaining. But the greatest question is, What was God doing? He led them around the long route because he was protecting them from themselves.

I want you to rethink your situation. Maybe God has you on the long route because he is trying to protect you from yourself. He is very aware of the timing of his blessings. And waiting on God's timing is something I tried to teach my daughter when she turned sixteen and wanted a car of her own.

GIMME, GIMME, GIMME

When my daughter Blair turned sixteen, she wanted a car and would not relent. Then her mother got involved. A few weeks before

Christmas, my wife, Jill, said, "You should buy Blair a car for Christmas."

"I don't have the money to buy a car. She'll have to wait."

"Wait" was not a word Jill wanted to hear, nor did Blair, because, two days later, they went up out of their own little Egypt prepared for battle. They had a battle plan to wear me down. They wanted me to call this dealership and that dealership, turning me into the mean guy who continually had to say no. Every time we passed a car lot, it would start. "Honey, why don't we stop and see what they have on the lot?" Jill would whine, and I'd keep both hands on the wheel and my eyes on the road. I'd shake my head and say, "We've already been over this, and the answer is no!" They were no match against my pharaonic nature.

But it didn't deter them. They came at me with a plague of car commercials. While we watched television at night, car commercials would break into our serenity, and the two of them would have a conversation intended for my ears.

"I think you'd like that car," Jill would say.

"No, it's a little too boxy. I want something sporty."

Jill would agree, and when a commercial came on that they both agreed would be the right car for her, Jill would say, "You need to tell your tightwad father to get you one of those."

I learned every jingle known to car dealerships because they turned the volume up, knowing they were getting on my nerves, knowing that those crazy jingles would get stuck in my mind. I never let on that I was singing the jingles at work. If they had known, they would have derived so much pleasure, so I sang them while I walked the halls at church and as I sat in my office with my feet on the desk, head thrown back and hands raised in car worship. Then, just like a good preacher, I attacked them from my recliner pulpit at home. I pooh-poohed every new sale, every rebate, and called them all phonies. I maligned the pretty girls who were slinging their arms, exposing all the new cars the camera could force into one frame.

The week before Christmas, things got worse. The topic of buying a car became a point of contention, and Blair and Jill's argument was justifiable. Blair needed a car. I understood that, but I let them know that this observation didn't change things.

"The timing is not right," I said.

I wanted Blair to wait for her desires patiently instead of whining and complaining and demanding. I wanted to see her persevere in waiting for a car.

THE FLUTTERING OF CHICKEN WINGS AND HER HANDS

The moment came when Jill and Blair surrendered their desire to buy a car. It was what I was hoping for. I was proud of them. They submitted to God's timetable of making Blair a car owner, and Jill decided I should get Blair some other gift to make up for the car that she wasn't getting.

"Well, what about a CD player?" I suggested.

"That will be fine. I'll get her some clothes and a new purse," Jill said with newfound excitement.

On Christmas morning, Blair sluggishly opened her presents. She was happy it was Christmas, but you could tell she still longed for the car. She ripped the paper off a present and looked inside to find a box full of wood blocks with a note. She pulled the note out, her face contorted in bewilderment, and read it out loud.

"Blair, I know it's not a CD player, but I thought you'd like this instead. Love, Dad."

Attached to the note was a matchbox car. She held it up, confused, and then opened it. She discovered a key and held it up in wonder.

"You might want to look outside," I said, helpfully.

They ran to the front door and flung it open. Then they screamed, danced on the tips of their toes, and fluttered their elbows like chickens in a barnyard. They ran toward a white Honda Civic parked out front and piled in, squealing loud enough to wake the neighborhood, while Blair turned every knob on the dash, her hands trembling wildly between each knob.

Then Jill asked, "How long have you had this car? Where have you been hiding it?"

"Oh, I don't know. I've been hiding it since December eighth in Bobby's garage."

"You've been hiding it in a garage! You mean you had this car in somebody's garage the whole time we've been begging for one?" Blair asked.

"Yep, the car has been in the garage waiting for this moment. When you thought there'd be no car, it was there the whole time."

Jill started beating on my chest with her fists, then she hugged me and kissed me.

Now, around our house when one of us is waiting for something to happen, we say, "The car is in the garage!" knowing this frees us from trying to make it happen. "What is faith? It is the confident assurance that what we hope for is going to happen. It is the evidence of things we cannot yet see" (Hebrews 11:1).

Maybe you are longing for something to happen in an area of your life. Chances are God has it "in the garage," waiting for the appointed time when he will present it to you. "So don't get tired of doing what is good. Don't get discouraged and give up, for we will reap a harvest of blessing at the appropriate time" (Galatians 6:9). God has an appointed time to bring the plans of our lives to fruition. So ask for strength, and leave the travel time to God, because the key to surviving an extended time in the desert is to make it a "passionate and contemplative crucible in which new life and spiritual wholeness can be birthed."[3]

THE TERRIBLE TICKING IN BETWEEN

The sun was going down on the Children of Israel's first week of freedom. They'd walked until their feet hurt and their stomachs rumbled. It had been an eventful week. The Exodus became a showdown. And Miriam sang while the Egyptian horses and their riders swirled beneath the sea. It was their first week under the stars, away from Egypt. Big sky country, oval at the edges. They stood in purple darkness, watching their water supply dribble away. The miles to go were long. Their dreams were being dashed against a reality that Moses may have delivered them from slavery only to kill them in the desert. Death had seemed like a possibility at the Red Sea, yet their fears were cast aside as God rescued them. The rumor mill was working again during a three-day march into the wilderness without water. Then God cursed them with forty years of the "terrible ticking in between." The funerals must have been daunting for Moses. The graves stretched seemingly forever out into the distance of time. And Moses, unnerved by it, sat down before the Lord and started writing what was on his heart: "Relent, O, Lord! How long will it be? Have compassion on your servants" (Psalms 90:13 NIV). This psalm is a plea for God's mercy. Moses probably penned it as a prayer to be used daily by the people in their tents or by the priests in the tabernacle.4

It was heavy, this work of God. But "Moses kept right on going because he kept his eyes on the one who is invisible" (Hebrews 11:27). So must we. Blessings lie beyond our sight.

CONSTRUCTION—
A WAY OF LIFE

Admitting You're Not Perfect and Never Will Be

MICHAEL W. SMITH DRIVES a white Land Rover. I know because I've been behind him in the carpool line. When I lived in Nashville, we both dropped our kids off at the same school. His kids would hug him and peck his cheek with a kiss, then jump out with their backpacks wagging behind them. I tried to stay away from him. I didn't want to get caught behind him or in front of him in the carpool line in my '70 four-door Nova with a faded hood. Not in my lime green hooptie; not in the slime mobile that oozed down the road in greasy lumps. When I picked up my daughter and her friend from school, they hid in the back seat until the school was out of sight.

One day the muffler fell off my car in a carpool line. We made the turn into the drop-off lane when suddenly it happened. The muffler hit the pavement. Sparks flew, heads turned, and we scraped to a halt. I jumped out and surveyed the exposed properties of disaster, noticing that my riders hadn't bothered to hang around to help. They exited the car as quickly as Elvis would exit a building and left me standing there exposed in all my ugliness—naked before parents, alumni, janitors, and teachers alike—as they gawked at the freak exposure of a muffler's fallenness.

We all hide our weakness, our darkness, our ugliness, and, just like that muffler, our fallenness. We hide because we are afraid that if the truth about us is known, people will think we don't belong on the journey to God's kingdom.

WE'LL GET THERE WHEN WE GET THERE

In their book, *The Art of Possibility*, Rosamund Stone Zander and Benjamin Zander postulate that a part of us speaks from "Measurement Central," the place where we perceive the world. We measure things. We contrast and compare. We look for ways to make sense of how we are doing as humans, as Christians, and the central way we understand our world is by measuring things. "That opinionated 'little voice in the head' is almost always speaking from Measurement Central. Life in the measurement world seems to be arranged in hierarchies: some groups, people, bodies, places, and ideas seem better or more powerful than others."[1]

They seem to be echoing what Paul said to the Corinthians, because nothing has changed in the world of measurements. We're still measuring ourselves against others. It's the game the world plays. It can't help itself. Measuring is in the very fibers of the world's foundation. And what we do with the data of our measurements is where the problem arises. Measuring is not bad. It's what we measure with and why that gives us problems.

When my brother and I asked the childhood question, "Are we there yet?" on family vacations, we weren't seeking measurement. If Dad would've said, "We'll be there in sixty-five miles," we would've been lost. We knew nothing of miles per hour. Dad had a pat answer: "We'll get there when we get there," which wasn't bad advice, come to think of it. It's the same advice given to the recipients of Peter's epistles. "Now we live with a wonderful expectation because Jesus Christ rose again from the dead. For God has reserved a priceless inheritance for his children. It is kept in heaven for you, pure and undefiled, beyond the reach of change and decay. ... It will be revealed on the last day for all to see"

(1 Peter 1:3–5). Peter adjusted their inner clocks to eternal time. They were measuring their problems with emotional reasoning—"I feel it so it must be true." It seemed as if nonbelievers were getting better treatment than the followers of Christ. This has always caused confusion, but Peter didn't try to explain it away. He pointed to the most important fact of life—eternity.

MISSING THE DANCE

Around Valentine's Day, my daughters' school in Nashville holds a father-daughter dance. I was no stranger to this dance. I'd attended plenty of times with Blair. It was nice. No big deal for an introvert. You go. You eat. You get your picture taken. You go home. The year Sloan started the first grade, things changed. Some wise guy in charge must have been bored with the whole proceeding because he called for a dance hop, a fifties extravaganza—a night howling with Wolfman Jack. And there was a dress code. Everybody had to dress as if they had stepped out of the fifties—leather jackets, white T-shirts, and poodle skirts. I hate dressing like a fraud because it makes a fraud feel even more fraudulent. You're out of control when you dress according to someone else's wishes. It leaves room for error. But I played the fraudulent part of dressing like and acting like Fonzie. I put on a white T-shirt two sizes too small, rolled up the cuffs on my jeans, and slipped on a pair of wing-tipped shoes.

The place was decorated to the tune of a fifties song. "Blue Suede Shoes" was setting the mood while Sloan led me through the crowd to where pictures were being taken behind a mock '57 Chevy. We sat in two classroom chairs behind the wooden '57 Chevy, looking as if we were cruising Sonic. We smiled, baring our teeth at a man who made us say "Elvis." Then he snapped the picture and said, "Next."

I moved slowly through the dance hop, stopping every now and then as Sloan chatted with a friend. Then I spotted him. He came through the door leading his daughter through the crowd as if she were a princess, the heir to some throne in another decade. Michael W. Smith was everything we all hope to be as a father—cool. I felt like a fraud. I was a fraud.

Sloan and I took our seats around folding tables decorated in boisterous colors with confetti splashed against the surface. We sat and ate hamburgers and french fries. Every now and then, I'd glance at Michael W. Smith. He was twitching to the music while he ate a hamburger. His arm was around his daughter, supporting her. I had both elbows on the table, feeling inadequate in a room full of CEOs and Christian music stars and producers who made up the private school's budget.

Sloan was having a good time. I could tell. Her hair was pulled back in a ponytail that was bobbing while she talked to one of her classmates. They were sharing her fries. Community had constructed around me, yet I kept to myself and avoided the conversations buzzing around me. Daughters were discussing poodle skirts, men were chatting about business deals or where they worked, but I was stone-faced silent, wishing I were at home in my recliner. Then everyone grew silent when someone announced a dance contest.

INSTRUMENT OF ELIMINATION

I failed to factor in one thing. I might have been dressed like Elvis, but I couldn't move like him. So I'm plastered to the back of my chair with a roller-coaster scared look on my face. One of the fathers was reading the dance contest rules over a makeshift PA system.

"The instrument of elimination will be a tap on the shoulder and a nod from our judges. The last couple standing will be the winners. ... Okay, everyone to the dance floor!"

Fathers and daughters pushed back their chairs and streamed onto the dance floor. I didn't move. So Sloan grabbed me by the hand and said, "Let's go, Dad."

I glanced at her, then glanced at the dance floor. I started sweating and breathing fast. Adrenaline started pumping. I looked toward the door.

"Dad?" Sloan said while tugging on my arm.

The fraudulent one was about to be killed on the dance floor. There would be no way to hide. The judges would be breathing down my T-shirt. Sloan put her hands on her hips and swung the poodle skirt to the left as she shifted her weight. Then her face became determined. She grasped my arm again and pulled. I could see the other fathers twirling their daughters. I could smell their sweat. I could hear their deep breaths.

I was at the edge of the dance floor when I looked over to see *him*. He was there, fully in the moment, a smile on his face. It would have been okay if we'd entered the dance floor beside the school nerd and her dad, but no, as fate had its moment, we were beside the "man" himself, Michael W. Smith, and the boy has some moves. John Travolta didn't have anything on him. He was swinging his daughter between his legs and spinning her around. It was an act of grace, and I smiled at ol' Smitty, looking him in the eyes. I even nodded a hello to him.

Then I danced. It was not really dancing. It was more like running in place. You talk about the inadequacy of having no rhythm. I had nothing that even resembled a cadence. Smitty would make a move with his daughter, and I would answer it with a spectacular high hurdle running motion and a nod and a smile. I crossed from cool to nerdy, all in one move on the dance floor. I felt guilt—the guilt of an inadequate father. Then I felt a tap on the shoulder. We were out.

THE FEAR OF THE TAP

I beat myself up for days. I started hiding out in the '70 Nova in the carpool line, wearing dark sunglasses and a Dale Earnhardt hat. I felt like a leper with three feet and a misshapen lip. I was the high-hurdler that got tapped.

Most of us live with the fear of the tap, the sense that at any minute God is going to tap our shoulders and call us out because of our weak performances. So to score ourselves—to see how we are measuring up against the Michael W. Smiths of this world—we make the wrong move and use the world's measuring system to measure our spirituality. Not that Michael W. Smith was measuring himself against others. He's not like that. The measuring was my own sick neurosis. I lived off the erroneous belief that spirituality is calculated and recalibrated as we compare ourselves with others. Paul comments, "I wouldn't dare say that I am as wonderful as these other men who tell you how important they are! But they are only comparing themselves with each other, and measuring themselves by themselves. What foolishness!" (2 Corinthians 10:12).

Paul refused to use the world's measurements to measure his apostolic call to preach. "But we will not boast of authority we do not have. Our goal is to stay within the boundaries of God's plan for us, and this plan includes our working there with you" (2 Corinthians 10:13). Paul worked off the boundaries of God's plan, not the world's measurements. This is the grand exchange—exchanging the world of measurement that compares us with each other for the boundaries of God's plan, which measures how deeply rooted our self-worth is in Christ.

It's a move away from the world of measurement and comparison, but that doesn't go away without a struggle. Our deep-seated inferiority complexes won't let us give up the measuring game. Without measurements, we feel hopelessly void. How do we know how we're doing? And if spirituality is about measuring, as some believe, then the church becomes the place where we get the job done. Church becomes a place of measurement and loses the power of transformation. We are transformed only when our minds stop measuring. "Don't copy the behavior and customs of this world," Paul admonishes, "but let God transform you into a new person by changing the way you think. Then you will know what God wants you to do" (Romans 12:2).

Some believe that God wants us to be perfect, and I've seen bumper stickers that read, "If you sin, you're not saved." I've wanted to flag one of the cars over and get a good look at a perfect person, but they're usually speeding by me so fast I can't get my hand up.

Paul says in Philippians 3:12, "I don't mean to say that I have already achieved these things or that I have already reached perfection! But I keep working toward that day when I will finally be all that Christ Jesus saved me for and wants me to be." I think the hardest thing for us to do is to sit in church week in and week out without trying to measure ourselves, whether it's with an inferiority complex or with an inflated ego. "To most of us, however, perfection seems impossible of fulfillment. 'Be not anxious' is a command most of us would like to be able to obey, but feel unable to do so."[2] When we fail at the perfection game in one area, we start competing in another. We swap one yardstick for another one, and usually this happens when people get involved in church. They don't know how to be part of a community without measuring themselves with others. The game of one-upmanship just takes on a different face. One yardstick is traded for another. I did this in the fourth grade.

4-H Clubs and Cat-Head Biscuits

My goal in the fourth grade was to flee math class, where measuring is game number one. I joined 4-H thinking I'd discovered a way out of measuring. It wasn't a popular organization with the boys in my social group. They scorned it, but not me. I saw it for what it was worth—a trip out of class. None of the boys I hung around with wanted to be a part of an organization that at its very roots was corrupted by geeks, or so we thought. I didn't care. It was a reason to be out of math class, but I discovered our 4-H club was not a hangout for losers. You couldn't attend and sit in the corner with your blue jean jacket over your head while slobber oozed out of the corner of your mouth.

In 4-H club you had to perform, in a category of choice, for some ribbons, which meant I had to choose. But having to compete wasn't what I had in mind. I could see right off that about three-quarters of the projects you had to be a part of looked like work, even though I did think twice about having a dairy cow. I knew I could milk that sucker and dust it for flies, but the problem with raising a dairy cow is the locale. We had no land in my subdivision. We had little white houses crammed into a small opening behind a strip mall that backed up to a creek. The water supply would be sufficient, but then you've got the grazing to worry about—and I knew my father wouldn't let me tie her to the wrought-iron post that supported the carport.

So I had to forgo the dairy cow and decided on bread making. I kid you not. I took one look at my competition—all girls with skinny frames. And I measured them. Sized them up. I knew my grandmother made biscuits that were out of this world, so I signed up for competition in bread baking. I called my grandmother that night and jotted down the recipe. I whipped those suckers up, placed them on a plate, and covered them with Saran Wrap.

The following day, I hid them in my locker. When they dismissed the 4-H clubbers, I stood up on my red Converse tennis shoes and gave the boys in math class a wicked smile and walked out. I retrieved my biscuits and tried to look invisible on my way to the 4-H meeting. I could hear chatter from the cafeteria. It was a moment of confusion. Was I a geek? Was I sure about this bread-baking contest? I knew I'd never be looked at in the same way again.

Then I saw them standing there. My competition—Abby, Melissa, June, and that dried-up Joanna. And in that moment, I realized why I was there. I was there to win! Who cared about getting out of math class? Yeah, I was playing the game, but the game just changed. I was into the game for the glory and the feel of victory. I'd been sucked into the contest. I placed my plate of biscuits next to theirs. They smirked. They talked out of the sides of their mouths with their hands hiding their insults.

At that moment, the contest taster rounded the rickety tables that doubled for a showcase and stopped at a plate. She peeled back the plastic wrap on Joanna's entry. She felt the texture of the biscuit and sniffed it as if it were a strange object recovered from a nursery school sandbox. Then she placed the biscuit in her ancient mouth, the mouth that made every 4-H bread maker tremble. She chewed. She scrunched her face as if she was surprised by its awfulness. She swallowed hard to get it down, while I tried to keep a poker face. Joanna wasn't doing so well with her own facial reactions as her face sagged under the weight of the bread autopsy report. It was not a good taste test.

The contest taster cleansed her palate with a shot of water and went through the usual taste test with my Mama Nell's biscuits. She inserted the biscuit into her moist mouth and then stopped, as if she'd heard a faint cry from the hall. Resuming, she rolled my biscuit back to her cavity-riddled molars and chewed with the delight of nine cats. Then she smiled at me, and I knew, oh, did I know. That blue ribbon was mine, baby! The girls had been defeated by a punk boy who was skipping math class. And for two consecutive years, I carried home the blue ribbon. They didn't stand a chance against my lard cat-head biscuits.

It's easy to get caught up in the game of winning blue ribbons. Even church can become just another place to measure ourselves against others. We quickly learn where the blue ribbons are being handed out. Then we turn our spiritual journey into a 4-H biscuit contest, believing that happiness and righteousness are just one blue ribbon away.

How do we get free from this need to compete in a world dominated by laws and rules and things that must be measured? One way to set ourselves free is to arrest the urge to live by the Should Syndrome, where you "conjure up a set of expectations of how you think things should be—or what others say they should be—and then measure yourself, without mercy, against it."[3]

When life is based on how it *should be*, we never get around to living the life that is ours. Life becomes a mere speculation that drives us to performance-based self-worth, which sets expectations on our performance in dance contests and achieving blue ribbons in a biscuit contest. The problem is not the desire to be in these contests, it's the feeling we come away with, even if we've won. It's the feeling of being a fraud.

In David Foster Wallace's short story "Good Old Neon," his protagonist feels trapped in what he calls a "fraudulence paradox."

> My whole life I've been a fraud. I'm not exaggerating. Pretty much all I've ever done all the time is try to create a certain impression of me in other people. Mostly to be liked or admired. It's a little more complicated than that, maybe. But when you come right down to it it's to be liked, loved. Admired, approved of, applauded, whatever. You get the idea.
>
> There was a basic logical paradox that I called the "fraudulence paradox" that I had discovered more or less on my own while taking a mathematical logic course in school. ... The fraudulence paradox was that the more time and effort you put into trying to appear impressive or attractive to other people, the less impressive or attractive you felt inside—you were a fraud. And the more of a fraud you felt like, the harder you tried to convey an impressive or likable image of yourself so that other people wouldn't find out what a hollow, fraudulent person you really were.[4]

Fraudulence is the feeling we have when we realize the distance between our supposed perfection and the way we really are. A fraud is a person who denies the distance, or pretends to deny the distance because he doesn't know what else to do. He feels like his efforts *should be* better.

THE MUSIC CITY MIRACLE!

After the father-daughter dance, I started working on my self-image problem. First I had to admit that a problem existed. It was hard for me to see anything inside worth loving. When I was dancing on the same floor with Michael W. Smith, I was trying to measure up to his strengths, which compounded my weaknesses. Ralph Martin says, of Paul's rebuttal in 2 Corinthians 10:12 about measuring ourselves against others, "In the game of self-praise, [Paul] retorts, I haven't the skill to play."[5]

Neither do I.

Self-denial is our way out of a fragmented, competitive world that we have created with our own egos. There will always be a civil war inside of us—the Law against the Spirit. Self-denial versus an ego trip. "Some people are hypocrites because they try to appear much better than they really are. Other people are hypocrites because, for some silly reason, they are afraid to allow that which is true and fine in them to stand revealed."[6] It's a fine line. We don't want to appear to be fraudulent people, but then again we don't want to hide out in a carpool line beneath sunglasses and a Dale Earnhardt ball cap.

Finding ourselves is a lifelong journey. Perfection can't be measured. Who knows, but my high-hurdle dance moves could be the way it's done in heaven. Maybe Gabriel and Moses and the one who leaned on Jesus' bosom and the one who stepped out of the boat and the widow with one mite are dancing at this moment in high-hurdle leaps. It could be a possibility, as all things are possible when we try to "allow that which is true and fine in [us] to stand revealed."

There's a teenager in my church who is mentally challenged. He talks with lisps and stuttered utterances. When he grows up, he wants to be an announcer for the Tennessee Titans. He knows Titan statistics better than the current Titans commentator, and one night while standing in the church foyer after the service, I asked him to act as if he were announcing a game. He did.

He chose the "Music City Miracle" play, when Kevin Dyson returns a Frank Wycheck lateral on a kickoff return seventy-five yards for a touchdown, lifting the Titans to a 22–16 victory in the AFC wild card playoff game over the Buffalo Bills. He had it all memorized, down to the finest detail. Who knows how many times he'd raced through it all in his mind? And in that foyer, it took on a life of its own. His voice was rising and falling with throat growls, and his mouth was making oval shapes while his tongue clucked the roof of his mouth, and he ended it in one long scream, "It's a mirrrrracle!" Then he smiled and caught his breath. And maybe his wish to be a commentator for the Tennessee Titans was somehow a way to be attached to a miracle, because he said, "Sometimes I wish I could wake up in the morning and be normal."

Don't we *all*?

YIELDING TO LIFE'S DEMANDS

How to Keep Your Sanity When Everyone Else Is Losing Theirs

JILL AND I WERE basement dwellers who refused to submit. Love was the only rule we desired, but love and an occasional candy bar will not get you through life.

The first year of our marriage, we moved into the basement of her parents' house, a logical first step to buying a condo in the suburbs of Franklin, Tennessee. We were nineteen and free. Lovers on the bottom floor taking one last run at preadulthood. Things would change. We knew this. Yet, we didn't know.

After we moved into the basement, Sanford, Jill's father, called me to the top of the stairs and said, "Robbie, I'm the head of the house and you will be head of the basement."

I thought it was his way of giving me free rein to live as I pleased in the basement, but I soon learned that the head of the house controlled the head of the basement. He had control of the thermostat upstairs, which regulated the whole house, and the head of the house was a descendent of Scrooge who rarely used his central heat and air system. He bragged about it being twenty-five years old and yet as cold as the day he moved in.

Every night after the local news, as we lay cool as cucumbers, we'd hear him get up over the sounds of "The Tonight Show" band. The boards above our heads would creak, and he'd ram the thermostat above 90 degrees. Then the dinosaur out back would puff one last breath of cool air, and we'd look at each other, roll our eyes into the next state, and kiss the fresh air good-bye. The head of the house had no mercy and slept all night with nothing stirring the air except his belittling snores, while we exhaled deep sighs, tossed on the bed, and yearned for the condo in the suburbs the way a child longs to get out of the backseat on vacations. We wanted freedom.

We were being persecuted by the head of the house. He was sweating us out! That was our take on things. Because when you can't understand why the top floor is making the bottom floor sweat, it raises doubts about the goodness of the top floor. But what can you do? Take control of your destiny? You bet. So one night we slipped upstairs and took control of the dinosaur. We woke it up and made it bellow all night, and did so for a whole month. When the electric bill arrived in the mailbox, the head of the house gave us an old-fashioned lecture about growing up with no A/C and sent us back to the basement to lick the sweat from our upper lips. We paid extra that month, and "yield" became the operative word.

YIELD IS NOT A HOUSEHOLD WORD

Yield is not a word that we keep on the tip of our tongue. We never get up in the morning and announce, "I'm going to yield today!" It doesn't happen. We never say to the person behind us in the grocery store line, "Go ahead, buddy. I'm yielding today."

Everyone yields to something. It's a law of the universe. Just ask the recipients of Peter's two epistles. As Christians, they couldn't understand why they had to yield to an authority figure like Nero, who torched Christians to illuminate his garden parties and covered them with the hides of wild beasts and fed them to the lions in the arena. They were being abused by the authority that was ordained to protect them, and it seemed unjust. It confused their theology. So Peter wrote his first epistle to realign their thoughts, to remind them that they were eternal beings on the way home: "There is wonderful joy ahead, even though it is necessary for you to endure many trials for a while" (I Peter 1:6).

The main theme of I Peter is endurance by yielding, which didn't offer any immediate relief for Peter's audience, but Warren Wiersbe believes, "Peter wrote to encourage them to be good witnesses to their persecutors, and to remember that their suffering would lead to glory."[1]

Our sweating in the basement was nothing compared to what they were suffering, but even though our suffering today is mild—especially in America—compared to theirs, it still creates thoughts of hopelessness and helplessness. And when Jill and I felt smothered in the basement, we'd escape to the local Waffle House—a breakfast specialty restaurant.

REDNECK EMERIL RECIPE

I like Waffle House's unique atmosphere. I like the way it smells like lard and bacon, waffles and sausage, coffee and hash browns. The place is breathtaking! Not breathtaking in the sense of beautiful, but breathtaking in the sense that there's only so much actual oxygen to go around. It's Marlboro country. No Benson & Hedges women in this joint. They smoke like men and talk loud and let out sweet groans when their orders are placed in front of them, and you best not play one of the three songs on the jukebox that isn't country or they'll prop you up against the jukebox after they break your bones. They probably wouldn't go that far, but stares may erupt and heads might turn.

I'm not looking down my pointed nose, because they're part and parcel of my star-studded bloodline. They're my redneck cousins that I'll never deny. If you sit in the Waffle House long enough, you'll hear a certain order being shouted to the short-order cook, because some old boy will blow in with cow muck on his boots and an appetite the size of Alabama, and he'll order a certain recipe for hash browns—scattered, smothered, and covered. It's a redneck Emeril recipe—hash browns scattered on the grill, smothered with onions, and then bam! covered with cheese. Not only is it an intoxicating recipe for hash browns, but it's the original recipe to overcoming our problems.

THE ORIGINAL RECIPE

1. Scatter the problems before you.

The first ingredient is the act of scattering our problems before us to see which ones carry eternal significance. In his first book, Peter scattered the eternal things out on the table before his readers. He acknowledged the way they'd been scattered in Roman provinces. He sympathized with their unjust treatment by Rome. It's a great introduction. He named the problem. He took the subject of being scattered and made it part of the solution. "I, Peter, am an apostle on assignment by Jesus, the Messiah, writing to exiles scattered to the four winds. Not one is missing, not one forgotten. God the Father has his eye on each of you" (1 Peter 1:1–2 MSG). He let them know that even though they were scattered, God hadn't forgotten or lost even one.

The recipients of the epistle had a civil war going on inside of them. They were living under Roman law while trying to live as citizens of God's kingdom. It's the harried wife syndrome, where she has to "be proficient in ten or twelve different occupations; or, stated otherwise, that she fill gracefully ten or twelve different roles,"[2] and eventually collapses because she takes on everything that comes her way and even asks for more. And Karen Horney, one of the most original psychoanalysts after Freud, says, "When a person is basically divided he can never put his energies wholeheartedly into anything but wants always to pursue two or more incompatible goals. This means that he will either scatter his energies or actively frustrate his efforts."[3]

Both were happening to Peter's audience, and as a result, they felt disconnected. They were tired of the same dull moment of pain that throbbed in their theology. *If God is so good, why are we suffering?* It's the adult version of the question "God, are we there yet?" only articulated through suffering. The difference between this question of suffering and the childhood question on a trip to the beach is where we place the emphasis. The childhood question places the importance of the trip on the expectation of what is to come—the future contains the reward. The adulthood question places the emphasis on the here and now: "When will I get the life I want, free of suffering?" There is no answer, except the one Peter gave: "Now we live with a wonderful expectation because Jesus Christ rose again from the dead. ... So be truly glad! There is wonderful joy ahead, even though it is necessary for you to endure many trials for a while" (I Peter 1:3, 6).

Numerous times, Jill and I wanted to go live in an apartment. We'd had enough of the cramped and stuffy conditions. Yes, we were ungrateful for the sacrifice and the hospitality that were being extended. We were brats. But being ungrateful whiners is not what made us think of quitting. When we succumbed to the belief that our situation was permanent, we lost sight of our "wonderful expectation," which was the condo in the suburbs. But to get there we had to travel through the basement. We submitted and stopped frustrating ourselves, because when our "attention is primarily directed to how wrong things are, we lose our power to act effectively."4

Once we stopped dwelling on what was out of our control, we were able to improve the environment in the basement. We scattered our problems out before us to discover which ones were under our control and needed immediate attention. Being hot was at the top of the list, so we focused our attention on how we might remedy the situation without driving up the electric bill.

The basement was one huge room that ran the length of the house. It had metal poles supporting the weight of the top floor. We put up two walls, boxing in a square at one end, using the poles as stabilizers.

By doing this, we trapped the cool air and used a fan to create new circulation. Our negative problem was transformed.

Paul was a master at separating the problems under his control from those that weren't. "And I want you to know, dear brothers and sisters, that everything that has happened to me here has helped to spread the Good News. For everyone here, including all the soldiers in the palace guard, knows that I am in chains because of Christ" (Philippians 1:12–13). He knew how to rearrange things to keep preaching while imprisoned. What can you rearrange to make life easier?

2. Smother the urge to limit life to this world only.

The second ingredient in the recipe of overcoming our problems is the act of smothering the urge to limit life to this world only, meaning we should be in the world but not of it. "There is wonderful joy ahead, even though it is necessary for you to endure many trials for a while" (1 Peter 1:6). Any type of failure or trial we go through must be viewed through the lens of eternity.

Jill and I continually smothered the sense of feeling trapped, smothered the urge to limit our life to the basement only. We had a "wonderful expectation" of a condo to look forward to. This thought smothered the urge to give up. When life is viewed through the lens of eternity, it makes this place temporary, and if it's temporary, then things will change, and so will our conditions. "And if we have hope in Christ only for this life, we are the most miserable people in the world" (1 Corinthians 15:19).

Martin Seligman, in his book Learned Optimism, writes, "Finding temporary and specific causes for misfortune is the art of hope. ... Finding permanent and universal causes for misfortune is the practice of despair." Elijah interpreted his situation as permanent and "sat down under a solitary broom tree and prayed that he might die. 'I have had enough, Lord,' he said. 'Take my life, for I am no better than my ancestors'" (1 Kings 19:4). Elijah felt things were permanent, which caused him to become morbid. He told himself things weren't going to work out.

Seligman believes that the way we communicate to ourselves about our circumstances is our "explanatory style." He believes we explain things to ourselves from a "yes" point of view or a "no" point of view. It's the "manner in which you habitually explain to yourself why events happen. ... An optimistic explanatory style stops helplessness, whereas a pessimistic explanatory style spreads helplessness."[5] Elijah was speaking from the pessimistic explanatory style.

Seligman believes that "people who give up easily believe the causes of the bad events that happen to them are permanent."[6] When their human efforts don't succeed, they give up, telling themselves that they don't have the strength to see it through.

Elijah explained his circumstances to himself in such a way that he felt no better than his ancestors. He talked himself into it. D. Martyn Lloyd-Jones writes, "The main art in the matter of spiritual living is to know how to handle yourself. You have to take yourself in hand, you have to address yourself, preach to yourself, question yourself. You must say to your soul: 'Why art thou cast down'—what business have you to be disquieted?"[7] Self-talk is not some psychobabble term. I believe we can operate as Paul did when he wrote, "Finally, brethren, whatever things are true, whatever things are noble, whatever things are just, whatever things are pure, whatever things are lovely, whatever things are of good report, if there is any virtue and if there is anything praiseworthy—meditate on these things" (Philippians 4:8 NKJV). This was Paul's explanatory style.

To find out what word you have in your heart, think about this picture: an apple with a knife stuck in it. Why is the knife sticking in the apple? Here are two possible reasons you may have come up with:

Positive possibility—"So you can slice it and eat it."

Negative possibility—"You're trying to cut out a worm."

The first is positive because you found the good relationship between the knife and the apple. You looked for the good. You said yes.

The second is negative because you found a negative relationship between the apple and the knife by believing that something brutal is taking place or you projected onto the apple the presence of a worm. Both negative. You said no.

Changing our explanatory style from no to yes transforms our behavior and gives us a perspective to live by. Paul was the master of living by yes. He interpreted his imprisonment as an opportunity to share the Gospel.

To be in the world but not of it is the key to overcoming our hopelessness. What does it matter if someone is getting more elaborate stuff and living like a heathen in the process? "Those in frequent contact with the things of the world should make good use of them without becoming attached to them, for this world and all it contains will pass away" (1 Corinthians 7:31). When we operate from a standpoint of eternity, we release our hold on why this world should nurse us to wealth. "The Day is coming when you'll have it all—life healed and whole" (1 Peter 1:5 MSG).

3. Covered by the story.

The third ingredient in the recipe of overcoming our problems is to understand that God's story, the "foreknowledge of God the Father, in sanctification of the Spirit, for obedience and sprinkling of the blood of Jesus Christ" (1 Peter 1:2 NKJV), is what covers us. Verse five of the same chapter says that God's children "are kept by the power of God through faith for salvation ready to be revealed in the last time" (1 Peter 1:5 NKJV). God's story of salvation in Jesus Christ is what covers us with God's protection. We have been sprinkled with Jesus' blood. Covered with it. Marked for eternity by the Gospel story. The story line of our lives is the "wonderful expectation" that one day our stories will finally bleed into the one story of Christ's death, burial, and resurrection.

The way to get the Gospel story to cover your story line is to partner with Christ in his suffering. "Instead, be very glad—because these trials will make you partners with Christ in his suffering, and afterward you will have the wonderful joy of sharing his glory when it is displayed to all the world" (1 Peter 4:13).

It's hard to understand how enduring trials will make us more Christlike. But the way to overcome most of our trials is to endure. It's the theme that we dislike in Peter's epistle, but Peter was trying to calm his readers' fears by telling them that they were covered by God's protection. "Not one is missing, not one forgotten. God the Father has his eye on each of you" (1 Peter 1:2 MSG).

Then Peter takes this protection further by using imagery drawn from Exodus 24:6: "sanctification of the Spirit, for obedience and sprinkling of the blood of Jesus Christ" (1 Peter1:2 NKJV).

In Exodus 24:6, "Moses took half the blood from these animals [young bulls] and drew it off into basins. The other half he splashed against the altar." He took the blood in the basins and slung it at the people, sprinkling them and covering them with forgiveness, reminding them that their sins were covered. They'd been made clean. It's the same imagery that David uses in Psalm 51:7 where he likens the remission of his sins to a priestly function of cleansing rites. Charles Haddon Spurgeon writes, "But David had also seen the priest take a basin full of blood, and dip hyssop [a plant] in it, and when the bunch of hyssop had soaked up the blood, he had seen the priest sprinkle the unclean person ... and then say to him, 'You are clean; you have admittance now to the worship of God.'"[8]

Today, we live under a different covering—"the sprinkling of Jesus' blood." Our former story line of sin has been canceled. The moment we blended our story line with the head of the house's story, our existence in the basement changed. No longer were we in a conflict with the top floor. Two stories become one, and out of this union, this yielding of our story into his, "one can expect divine help."[9] No longer were we in a conflict with the top floor. We'd partnered with a force greater than ourselves. We'd aligned with him and began a new journey. Two stories became one.

A BULLET HOLE

On Saturdays, the head of the house would invite us up for breakfast. He'd get his griddle out from under the cabinet, plug it in and grease it up with butter. Then he'd make pancakes while telling stories of the way it used to be around there, back before I was even thought of, back before he realized there would be a son-in-law living in the basement with his daughter. He'd flip pancakes while sausage sizzled, and he'd tell about the time when Jill's grandmother, Mrs. Moore, lived with them after her husband died. She didn't like being left alone. It scared her. So the head of the house, wanting to make a lasting impression on how great a son-in-law he was, displayed a pistol that would keep her safe if she were there by herself. He palmed it, turning it over as if he'd caught a fish and wanted to see the colors of the fins and the movement of the gills. It was supposed to be a quick lesson in proper gun handling and safety, and when Mrs. Moore asked him if it was loaded, the head of the house said, "I've got the safety switch on. Watch." He pulled the trigger and a bullet shot past Mrs. Moore, into the cabinet, exited the countertop, went through a cake on the counter, and then lodged itself in the wall.

"It's right here," the head of the house said, pointing to a section of the wall above the counter. "We covered the hole with wallpaper, but it's right here."

I laughed.

He shot back a sly grin.

Then I offered, "I bet it scared her to death!"

Another sly grin. Then, "Yeah, she never wanted to see that pistol again."

The head of the house would tell these stories nonstop while he loaded my plate with pancakes, taking a breath every now and then to ask me if I wanted more, and I'd motion with my hand as if to say, "Bring it on. Load it up. Keep 'em coming," and he would. Then he'd start another story about some other wild escapade of being in the navy, about sailing to Japan, about how he could still remember the Japanese language, and he'd spout off a few words.

I looked forward to those moments on Saturday mornings when the head of the house included the head of the basement in the telling and retelling of his stories that made up the hodgepodge of his life. The basement didn't seem so bad. I knew there'd come another Saturday when we'd no longer be basement-dwellers. I knew the logical step to the condo in the suburbs went through his story and made up mine. As Frederick Buechner says, "You fashion your story as you fashion your faith, out of the great hodgepodge of your life—the things that have happened to you and the things you've dreamed of happening. They're the raw material of both."[10]

Those breakfast moments opened a wide space in my heart that allowed me to accept the suffering of being the head of the basement with no control over the thermostat. And when the telling and retelling of God's eternal story merges with the here and now, something happens. At first it's difficult to recognize our story in the eternal story. Then, as the story gets told and retold, tiny splinters of his suffering integrate into our suffering. And recognizing Christ's suffering inside our stories is when we emerge out of our own. It's our first step into eternity. It's what Jack Kerouac means when he says, "I was so interested in the opera that for a while I forgot the circumstances of my crazy life and got lost in the great mournful sounds of Beethoven and the rich Rembrandt tones of his story."[11]

And when we hear the Gospel story for the first time or the five hundredth time, we forget the circumstances of our crazy lives. Because there's something in the way God abandoned his own Son, flashing his vulnerabliity at the Cross, integrating His story into our story, delivering us from the one mournful question, "Why have you forsaken me?"

GOING OUR OWN PRIDEFUL WAY

There Is a Road That Leads to Destruction

THERE WAS A WRONG way and a right way—two roads diverged in a weedy lawn, and I chose to rip up almost all the grass in my front yard. I got down on my hands and knees and just started grabbing weeds and clover and crabgrass by the hair of their heads and yanked them right out. I've been living in my present house for six years. When I moved in the grass looked like something Tiger Woods would tee off on. Now it's pathetic. Just ask ChemLawn. They drove by and condemned my yard. They left on my doorknob a flyer that included a full report about what was wrong with my lawn. It was no clean bill of health. I needed weed and feed, among other things.

So, feeling embarrassed, I threw the report in the trash and tried to forget that I'm not a green-thumbed lawn boy. Then the ChemLawn guy started calling my house two to three times a day. The phone would ring and his nasty little name would pop up on my caller ID screen. And sometimes at night, when the house was quiet and holy, when "Survivor" was on television, the phone would ring, and when I checked the caller ID display, it was the ChemLawn man. It went on for two weeks. The guy was relentless. No matter how

many times I ignored his calls, he was back like a crack addict need-
ing a hit, ringing in my ear like I was the dealer. Finally, I'd had
enough and I picked up the phone and said in a dull voice, "Hello."

"Mr. Stofel, this is ChemLawn. Did you get the packet of information I left on your door with the report on your yard?" he asked quickly,
before I could hang up.

"Yeah, I got it, and I'm not interested."

"Well, wait a minute, Mr. Stofel. Hang on there," he said with a
high-spirited green thumb in his voice. "Just let me explain."

"I told you I'm not interested." Then I accentuated it with a little
minister finesse, just in case he knew who I was. "Thank you for calling." Then I hung up, and it felt good.

But the ChemLawn man had tainted things. Every time I looked
at my front lawn, I pictured him in his green shirt, bent down in the
grass on one knee, while the clipboard rested on the other. I imagined him touching, even violating my grass, judging me, measuring
his green thumb against mine. So I went out one late Saturday afternoon and whipped my grass for everything that was every wrong
with it.

Within an hour, I had massive piles of weeds on the sidewalk, and
I felt the hot stares of my neighbors. They clustered across the street,
acting as if they were lounging, chatting, socializing, but I knew I was
the sideshow, the bearded woman, the midget with two heads. I knew
they were watching me, jeering at me, but I never acknowledged them.
I crawled and I yanked and piled the weeds up higher on the sidewalk,
and this is when Jill came home and took one look at the piles and
exclaimed, "Robbie, you're pulling up all the grass!"

I was defensive and emphatically denied doing such a thing and
never slowed down. I was on a mission to prove the ChemLawn man
wrong. How dare he insult my manhood of lawn care! I'd show him. He'd
drive by in his "the grass is greener on my side of the fence" green truck,
and he'd call me back.

"Mr. Stofel, the ChemLawn guy here. I just want you to know you did a heck of a job there on your weed problem. I apologize about the bad report card."

"Oh, don't mention it," I'd say.

Then he'd say, "How did you do it? I mean, everyone in your neighborhood has been calling me thinking I made your yard green and luscious, and I'm in a pickle. Will you just jump on the truck and go around the neighborhood and give me some pointers?"

"Aw, you just need to do a little bit of weed pulling here and there," I'd say.

AMERICAN LAWN IDOL

I've never been one to look at other people's grass. I couldn't care less if you had weeds or planted seed the first of spring. Yards don't generally bother me, but once my faults were pointed out, I started judging other people's yards. I was Simon Cowell and every man and woman on the block was a contestant in my "American Lawn Idol" competition.

As I drove out of the neighborhood, I would belittle my neighbors and call down the ChemLawn man on their scraggly yards. *How dare the ChemLawn guy come to my house when this guy's yard looks like a dandelion field!* I wanted to make up my own report cards and hang them on the neighbors' doorknobs while they were working. "Let them come home to this!" I'd say.

Before you accuse me of being melodramatic, let me explain. The reason I was upset was because I felt he was judging my green thumb. I've got hang-ups. I don't do well under ridicule, and the ChemLawn guy walked innocently into a front lawn filled with land mines. I was the one with the predisposition to criticism, which exacerbated my shame.

UNDER THE GREEN THUMB

I view life from center stage, just as you do. "We all have the tendency to perceive ourselves as the lead actor of a play and to judge other people's behavior exclusively in reference to ourselves."[1]

Everyone's vying for the lead role, and when ChemLawn critiqued my yard, I took it as a hostile act. It wounded my self-esteem to think that my lawn may not be up to the standards of other yards in the neighborhood. I could've denied it—and did deny in the beginning; I mean, I had been the leading lawn boy in my neighborhood growing up. My Converse tennis shoes were permanently stained green. No one was faster behind a mower. But now I'm not that particular about my yard. Don't get me wrong—I'm not condoning my denial, but it isn't worse than someone striving for perfection, thinking he can really beat the curse of the earth with a Briggs & Stratton 2.5-horsepower engine spinning a dull blade. This is what's so sad about the Pharisee in Jesus' parable. He thought he could beat the system with an overwrought religion.

Then Jesus told this story to some who had great self-confidence and scorned everyone else: "Two men went to the Temple to pray. One was a Pharisee, and the other was a dishonest tax collector. The proud Pharisee stood by himself and prayed this prayer: 'I thank you, God, that I am not a sinner like everyone else, especially like that tax collector over there! For I never cheat, I don't sin, I don't commit adultery, I fast twice a week, and I give you a tenth of my income'" (Luke 18:10–12).

One-upmanship is a lonely road that leads to destruction, because everyone is either above us or below us. There is no middle ground for snobs and Pharisees. They try to protect themselves from being contaminated by those below while elevating themselves to center stage.[2]

The Pharisee believed the only one more superior than himself was God, and this explains why he worked so hard to be righteous. To him, perfection was obtainable, and the childhood question, "Are we there yet?" turned into a way to judge others and put them down: "I'm already there and you're not." Snobbery at its best.

WHEN TRUTH BECOMES A WEAPON

Snobs will use truth as a weapon to keep you below them, or they'll despise those above them whom they perceive are holding them down.[3]

This is where anger comes in, because all of us are either below or above other people. This is why I gave up on the yard thing. I was outmanned and outmaneuvered. The guy across the street has his own personal lawn boy. He details the yard down to the small clover, which is probably a four-leaf clover knowing this guy's luck. You can't compete with that. He'll always be superior. The haves and the have-nots are a reality of life. Jesus said, "The poor you will always have with you." And that's okay with most of us because it means someone will always be below us. No one wants to be on the bottom of the food chain, which is strange considering Jesus also said that the last will be first. You'd think we'd be running over each other to be last. "You go ahead." "No, you go first," we should be saying. Sure, it would make the world a crazy place. We'd never get through the first red light. But who cares?

When you come right down to it, the most basic element of every life is selfishness, which produces anger when someone tries to push us down where Jesus said we should be in the first place. Life is a continual rise in the wrong direction. No wonder we feel "wronged." And I felt "wronged." I saw the ChemLawn man as being hostile toward my capability as lawn boy. *How dare he speak against my yard!* I thought. I personalized his attempts to get my business. I viewed his truth as a weapon.

The Pharisee presented his prayer as if he were the lead actor, sinless from birth, and this is why we love Jesus when he gouges the

Pharisees with parables. He attacked the Pharisee's worthiness, and the "Jewish leaders wanted to arrest him for using this illustration because they realized he was pointing at them" (Mark 12:12). The Pharisees viewed the world as a stage for their one-act play, and when their position in society was challenged, they felt wronged, picked on, and they became indignant. Their reaction to perceived interference was to mobilize an attack. "They wanted to arrest him, but they were afraid" (Matthew 21:46).

I need to learn that people aren't trying to attack me. I'll admit it—I need to get off center stage and stop being a fraud. I was knocked down a few notches in the neighborhood pecking order of lawn-boy greatness, and it made me mad. I went through Aaron Beck's "stages in the development of hostility"[4] and pounded each one as I mobilized an attack against myself.

Event → Distressed → "Wronged" → Anger → Mobilize to Attack

My anger was not the first feeling I had when I retrieved the ChemLawn report card from my door. It was only a symptom. I know now that I should've pinpointed the event that caused the distress and then debated whether or not it was a valid reason to be upset. *Was the ChemLawn man trying to make me feel inferior, or was he trying to get my business?* There's a huge difference.

CODE GREEN!

M. Scott Peck says neurotics drive themselves crazy, while psychotics drive everyone else crazy, and whichever one you think I might be, it can't be any worse than what I feel. I know my CPR treatment for the front lawn was a tad bit over the top. A good weed-and-feed chemical at the local hardware store would've worked. The ChemLawn man suggested it on his report card, and my first question should've been, "Am I being offended or empowered?" But who can see truth when it wounds? This is the problem. Someone once said that our problems can become our teachers. The hard part is admitting our deficiencies and then taking action to correct them. This is what I like about Moses—the man was real. There's a scene in Exodus 2 where Moses was on the run. He was a fugitive escaping to Midian, desiring a lonely life away from the limelight of Egypt, and ended up sitting on the edge of a well surrounded by seven beautiful women who were drawing water. Every time they filled their buckets, the thug-shepherds would "come and chase the girls and their flocks away" (Exodus 2:17).

Every morning, the same old routine for the girls: Up at 4 A.M. In the field by 5:00 to pick up the empty buckets resting on their sides. Then the laborious walk to the well, which produced frustration. Water was drawn, then stolen. Their goal was thwarted, which probably produced frustration, and if we subject these girls to Beck's "stages in the development of hostility," it would probably look like this:

Theft of water → Distressed → "Wronged" → Anger

Notice that I left out the last stage, which is "mobilizing to attack." Their anger never discovered its ventilation system. It was all bottled up inside. They felt helpless. Even their father had lost hope. "When the girls returned to Reuel, their father, he asked, 'How did you get the flocks watered so quickly today?'" (Exodus 2:18).

Most likely, they'd chosen passivity or, better yet, their father chose it. Where was this guy? Why wasn't he there helping his daughters? I know he was a priest, and like most preachers, he was probably flabby from too many trips to Denny's and made of the stuff of cowards. I'm no different. Who likes confrontation? But our frustration will not subside unless we confront the source. Problems won't go away by closing our eyes. Reuel had his eyes shut.

When anger is turned inward, it's a different kind of "mobilization to attack." It's an internal attack that diminishes our ability to cope. "When our attention is primarily directed to how wrong things are, we lose our power to act effectively."[5]

I've spent a lifetime mobilizing attacks against myself.

MOSES' FINAL EXAM

Then one day, as the shepherd-thugs are doing their thing, up walks a man who looks like Charlton Heston. He approaches the well and sits down, taking in the girls' daily frustrations, while wetting his cracked lips. He's stumbled into the final exam on anger management, and the bonus question is: *Will you beat these guys up or handle it responsibly?* Because frustration can lead to a healthy confrontation or it can lead to aggression. We must choose, and in Exodus 2:17, in that moment of decision, "Moses came to their aid, rescuing the girls from the shepherds." Yet the question remains: Did he respond in anger? True, he'd killed a man, but before we convict Moses of aggravated assault, what makes us think he used anger and aggression? Sure, offenders are hard to rehabilitate. We could take that view, but maybe his life turns around at this moment. Maybe he handles it with the correct tone, as the girls crack a justified smile. "Listen, guys, the game is over. From now on, you have to come through me if you want the girls' water."

It may have happened this way because the shepherds thought he was an Egyptian, and who wants to fight the law? And don't forget, he married one of the girls, and no matter how desperate she may have been, who wants to marry a man with a temper?

Life is frustrating, and it's hard to handle correctly when emotions get in the way. Sometimes our situations call for gentle confrontation. Here's a good formula to use:

Confrontation – an Emotional Charge = Alleviated Frustration

MR. BROWN THUMB

The day after I pulled the weeds out of my yard, the neighbor whose stare was the hottest on my bent back took my wife aside and asked, "What was your husband doing to the yard yesterday?"

"He was pulling up all the grass," she said.

"That's what I thought, too," the neighbor said.

As Jill told me about the conversation with the neighbor, I heard their chuckles slip into the breeze—little tee-hees and huh-uhs and choreographed head nods. I despised their holier-than-thou attitude that was trying to make me a second-class lawn boy with a brown thumb.

A few days later, while in the garage, I discovered an old bottle of crabgrass killer the last owner had left behind. A problem existed before me. I was not the originator of the weeds, which was proof that I'm not rotten to the core. The reality is that being judged and found wanting isn't bad; it just takes a lifetime to get over. I should've stopped and asked, "Is this an indictment against me or is someone trying to help?" If we can interject this question into every relationship, whether at work, home, or church, then we will be able to diffuse some of our anger. When we react to circumstances according to our predispositions, then anger will be the result.

My predisposition to low self-esteem immediately took the report card on my yard to mean I was not worthy to have a yard, that I wasn't very responsible. When an external event fits a particular belief, it will activate that belief, making it personal.[6] I believed that "a weedy yard is a sign of failure." The reaction was shame. It triggered feelings of being unworthy, which can translate into anger toward the person who exposed you. And it makes you feel as if he is saying, "I've arrived and you are lacking." It feels like a push down the ladder of success, and when an event triggers a faulty belief, the result is an overreaction.

Event: A Bad ChemLawn Report Card → Faulty Belief: Condemnation
→ Overreaction: Anger and Hurt

It translates to our spiritual life when some event triggers a faulty belief about God. When a tragic event takes place, those who see God as omnipotent will doubt his goodness. "If God were good, then this wouldn't have happened."

Tragic Event → Faulty Belief: God is not a good and
powerful God → Overreaction: Doubt

We've all been at this juncture, where we doubt if there really is a destination point on the journey. The childlike question becomes an indictment: "God, you are never there when I need you."

Os Guinness writes, "But if our picture of God is wrong, then our whole presupposition of what it is possible for God to be or do is correspondingly altered."[7]

This is why it's important not to overreact. Step back. Debate the logic, not the feelings. Challenge the belief you hold about God. Is it correct? Study Scripture to find out. Don't go on emotional reasoning as I did. Discover how faulty beliefs of God predispose a reaction to certain events.

The Pharisee in Jesus' parable believed he was justified by his great works, and he looked down his nose at the tax collector and said, "I thank you, God, that I am not a sinner like everyone else, especially like that tax collector over there!" (Luke 18:11). He had a faulty view of righteousness, because Jesus ended his parable by stating, "I tell you, this sinner, not the Pharisee, returned home justified before God" (Luke 18:14).

When it comes to eternal righteousness, there's a level playing field. The wrong way is to believe we can work our way to heaven. The correct way is the narrow path that leads through the Cross.

THERE WILL BE NO LAWN BOYS IN HEAVEN, I HOPE

There will be no lawn outside my mansion in heaven. I'm sure God has tipped off my builder, "Make his yard a parking lot." And on Saturdays, I'll get out the garden hose and wash down my yard, and I pray the ChemLawn man is my neighbor. I hope it drives him eternally nuts.

WE'LL LEAVE THE LIGHT ON FOR YOU

When Getting Out of Bed Is Harder Than Getting In

THE BATHROOM DOOR FLEW open and a karate move of aston-ishing agility dropped something at my feet. Then as quickly as it opened, the door slammed. For a nanosecond, I saw the object before it morphed. POP! My ears were ringing, but I could hear laughter out-side the door. I opened it, revealing three teenagers.

I remained calm and planned my revenge. I had three days. It was the second day of a week-long youth retreat in Florida. I was their youth leader. I was the target. I didn't get mad—I got even. In revenge you always want to measure the harm done to you, then multiply it by 663 times the firepower. I measured my retribution and laid it out where I could get to it. Then one of the kids played into my hands. He was the ringleader. Take him out and you've squelched the rebellion. He stepped into the bathroom while his buddies lay on the bed watching televi-sion. I pulled out my "bazooka." They jolted upright when they saw the mere strength of the revenge factor. Wicked smiles crossed their faces.

I shot back my own wicked smile.

It was a fifty-pack, small potatoes, less than the recommended revengeful firepower, but I didn't want to kill him, just maim him for the rest of the trip. I tugged on the bathroom door. The boy wasn't too bright. He hadn't locked it. I lit the fuse, flung the door open, and threw in the fifty-pack of firecrackers. But before the pack hit the target, my teenage subject slammed the door, knocking the pack back out onto the carpet in the room, where I stood in true cartoon character fashion with my fingers in my ears. No stopping the explosion now. The entire pack went up in flames and then formed a mushroom cloud of smoke under the smoke alarm. An atomic blast that devastated nostril hairs and eliminated any brain cells I may have had at the moment. Then the smoke set off the alarm. It screeched its message to the world while we waved our hands to clear the smoke. We covered our faces with our hands, creating homemade gas masks, but it didn't help. We threw open the door and smoke billowed out as if Cheech and Chong were in the room, but we weren't potheads celebrating smoke. No, we were pranksters who suddenly realized that smoke signals were being sent to the maid four doors down. "Close that door quick," I yelled. "We don't want to get in trouble with hotel management."

The door slammed and a terrified teenage prankster spread-eagled against the door—his mouth agape, teeth glimmering in the fallout of the firecracker blast. His eyes caught my eyes, and he realized I was terrified, too. So he said, "What are we going to do?"

I didn't have the foggiest idea.

Then someone knocked on the door.

"Stand back," I said, opening the door as if nothing had happened in our war zone. I stood there with a Dudley Do-Right grin, facing hotel housekeeping.

The maid mistook me for a teenager. (It may have been the smoke, but it was probably my cute baby face.) She said, "Where is your leader?"

Well, what was a youth leader to do?

I said, "I have no idea."

She stormed off down the hall in search of a leader who was standing in front of her. I shut the door to find three teenage boys staring at a huge hole in the carpet, as if an alien aircraft had landed and left its mark on the earth.

"Wicked," one boy said.

"You're in big trouble," another boy said.

"You lied to the maid," the last boy said with big brown eyes of disbelief.

It was true! I was a convicted liar who had a crime scene to clean up. There was no time to think about integrity or consequences. Revenge had backfired.

The agenda for the Valdez firecracker spill cleanup was to (1) save face, (2) make it look like nothing was wrong on the inside of our room, (3) convince everyone that it was just a malfunctioning smoke alarm. The cleanup was basically a cover-up. I became a spin doctor willing to go to great lengths to protect my image, and I skirted the boundaries of integrity to save my hide.

LYING THROUGH FALSE TEETH

I was aware of it the next day after the guilt of a successful cover-up. We'd dodged the hotel bullet. All I could think about, though, was that mushroom cloud of smoke. Every wave that crashed onto the beach was a cloud of smoke engulfing the smoke alarm. My success at covering up our misdeed did not lessen the guilt. The guilt had to go somewhere. I thought about blaming the teenagers. They started it! Then I thought about escaping. Maybe go down to Tijuana for a few days. But I was leaning more toward denial. It seemed easier. I would hide out at the pool behind sunglasses and go up every hour to see if the carpet had grown back together like Bermuda grass. It didn't. That's when I realized I had to get out of bed.

Getting out of BED
    Blame
    Escapism
    Denial

Getting out of BED is taking responsibility for our actions instead of blaming others, escaping from the problem, or denying there is a problem.

Getting out of the BED of

1. Blame—it's projecting onto others what I should take responsibility for.

"Don't point your finger at someone else and try to pass the blame!" (Hosea 4:4).

I could've blamed the teenager who started the fireworks fight. "Look what you made me do!" It would've been easy to project onto him the reasons for my boneheaded move. But there was no one to blame but myself. I was the adult. I was the leader. I was thirty years old, old enough to know better.

Harry Emerson Fosdick once said, "Conscience is easily drugged with self-justifications."[1] Blame is a self-justifying tendency to project onto others the guilt we don't want to feel. The classic example is when Adam said to God, "It was the woman you gave me who brought me the fruit, and I ate it" (Genesis 3:12). And blame has been happening ever since. If disobedience is the first sin in the Garden, then blame is the second. Blame is what Jesus took for us at the cross. All of our blame rested on his shoulders. He took the wrath of God for us.

No one can work his way to heaven, but a person who willfully projects his blame onto others will lose out in the end because his soul is being dwarfed. His potential is not reached. C. S. Lewis writes, "When a man is getting better, he understands more and more clearly the evil that is still left in him. When a man is getting worse, he understands his own badness less and less."[2]

To get out of BED, we have to stop playing the blame game. We should acknowledge the badness we feel in our conscience, then make a choice.

LUGGAGE OF GUILT

While I sat on the beach and curled my toes in the sand, I felt convicted. Carrying the guilt was a burden. "My guilt overwhelms me—it is a burden too heavy to bear" (Psalm 38:4). The psalmist was under the burden of guilt, hauling it to and fro, and, like a bad piece of meat that grows larger as it is chewed, guilt grows at the rate of every thought you give it. Guilt is heavy. Plus, it's not as if you need something else to carry. A heavy class load in college is enough. The workload that keeps you out of town or keeps your back bowed with overtime is enough. Carrying the load of parenthood is certainly enough. God knows that we don't need more things to carry. "Today's trouble is enough for today" (Matthew 6:34). If God doesn't load us down with tomorrows, then why do we allow ourselves to be burdened with yesterday's mistakes? Don't carry into today what you can leave behind in yesterday. The gift of forgiveness is the ability to know what to leave behind.

Burdens can be picked up and put down, which means we can choose what we carry. Acknowledging guilt is one thing; allowing it to sink you into regret is another.

I knew thinking guilty thoughts wouldn't change things. So I marched myself into the hotel office and confessed my sin. I confessed to letting off a pack of fifty firecrackers. I told them about the hole in the carpet. I admitted that I'd lied to the maid. They batted their eyes in disbelief and horror. One smirked. But I felt free. Refreshed!

Hotel management promised to check things out and get back to me. They took down my name, address, phone number, and church affiliation.

Now that the guilt was gone, I remembered the consequences—an unhappy deacon board with a treasurer who would freak out when he got the hefty bill, even though I had every intention of paying it. This is when I reconsidered going to Tijuana.

ESCAPE FROM FREEDOM

It's easier to run from problems than face them, but eventually running will tire you out. Ask Jonah. Ask John or Mark. Maybe Judas Iscariot. Sometimes me. Although we can't escape ourselves, we try. Some escape into drugs. Some into porn. Some shop. Others eat. A few go to Disneyland. I've been there, too. But the bad thing is that self tends to follow and linger after the rush of the escape. The Prodigal Son sought freedom and found the bondage of a pigsty. Gomer became a wayward preacher's wife, seeking freedom in other men's arms. Then there's the Gaderene demoniac. He kept breaking the chains that held him from freedom. But he didn't have anywhere to go. No wardrobe. He could not escape his demons, and neither can we, unless we face them. What a deceiver is escape.

Getting out of the BED of
2. *Escapism—its running from problems instead of facing them.*

"'Run for your lives!' the angels warned. 'Do not stop anywhere in the valley. And don't look back! Escape to the mountains, or you will die'" (Genesis 19:17).

Sometimes we feel that we'll die unless we escape to the mountains or put the "Do Not Disturb" sign on our door. Aloneness means no responsibility—just care of ourselves. It's the reason we run. It's not willing detachment as Jesus did to spend time with the Father. Escapism is an inner compulsion to break free from responsibliity. It is avoidance. But we can't avoid pain by escaping. There are many ways to escape. One that I'm familiar with is escaping into the problems and pain of others so you won't have time to feel your own pain.

AND THEN CAME ONE OF THOSE MOMENTS

I opened a home for troubled teens a half mile from the Titans' stadium in Nashville. Two blocks from the projects. The program required three months of residence, counseling, and follow-up guidance. One of my first troubled teens was sixteen and the product of a mother on crack cocaine. His progress was good until he received a call informing him of his mother's death.

The funeral was held on a Tuesday. The sun was out. A few clouds had gathered, along with a handful of people. My troubled teenager wore a pair of sunglasses he found while rummaging through his mother's apartment. Oval lenses with blue tint. A little too broad for his face, but he sat there at the grave with his head down and those sunglasses perched on his angular nose. He was staring at the green indoor-outdoor carpet put down for the family. I knew he was probably looking for some kind of light, some kind of sense, something to believe in, something that might be found while he was wearing his mother's sunglasses.

The week after the grave site scene, he started escaping. It was like the place was Alcatraz and I was the warden. He found ways out that I couldn't track down to secure for future attempts. He was an escape artist, running into the wild hills of Hendersonville, a community north of Nashville. And I chased him. Found him. Almost had him. Lost him. That was how my days were being filled. I'd sit in the apartment of the relative who had custody of him, because it was a known fact that he was refueling and taking a quick shower. So I'd hide inside, sitting on the couch in the dark, while the relative was at work. Then I heard him at the door. I slumped down in the couch. I wanted him to shut the door, and then I'd jump him.

The doorknob turned. I heard the screen door catch his backside. Then the door opened, and light came rushing into the darkened room. He didn't see me. My breathing was heavy. The door shut and the doorknob clicked. He saw me. I dove. Missed him. He ran up the stairs, slipped on a couple of steps, and started digging with his hands. He made it to the top and took a left, and I came running into the bedroom after him. He was gone. Vanished. Poof! Then the breeze touched the curtains. He'd jumped out the second-story window, and I pushed back the curtains and watched him run. I watched him gallop—long strides with his long legs, and, in that moment, I wanted him to run. I wanted him to get away. I longed for him to find a new place to live free from this destiny that was dealt him to have a dead crack addict for a mother. I wanted to shout, "Run, boy, run! Don't look back! Run and keep running until you get free from this world." And then I realized what I was really chasing—my shadow-self. I'd projected onto another that which I could not face in myself. It's what we hate in others and hate in ourselves at the same time. I was trying to fix the boy so I wouldn't have to take a look inside my own warped psyche.

I don't know why, but the experience touched a feeling deep inside me. It was the feeling that tricked me into starting a home for troubled youth in the first place. I was that kid once—rebellious, hell-bent, and clueless that a God would even care. Eighteen before anyone told me God loved me. I grew up scared of God.

I watched the boy run, halfheartedly wanting to join him, but no one has ever escaped responsibility. Wordsworth calls responsibility the "Stern Daughter of the Voice of God."[3]

That's why I stopped chasing him and called the police, who caught him three streets over. They threw him in the back of the squad car, and he stared out the side window, his hands cuffed behind his back. His face strained as if to say, "You dirty little youth home worker with your high ideals. Stop messing up my life of running." But it's better to learn early that you can't outrun the darkness inside of yourself. At some point you have to face it, talk about it, accept the hand that has been dealt you, and play it the best you can. Let the light of God come in and blast away those shadow-selves.

I realized I needed to face the darkness in myself, the darkness that had me chasing a delinquent boy in Hendersonville in the first place. And that's when I closed the doors to the youth home and walked away. Because what that boy needed was not some guy who was trying to undo his own terrible childhood by opening a youth home.

Getting out of the BED of escapism means we stop running and face the hurt of our past. We expose darkness to the light: "This is the message he has given us to announce to you: God is light and there is no darkness in him at all. So we are lying if we say we have fellowship with God but go on living in spiritual darkness. We are not living in the truth. But if we are living in the light of God's presence, just as Christ is, then we have fellowship with each other, and the blood of Jesus, his Son, cleanses us from every sin" (1 John 1:5–7).

After I closed the doors to the youth home, I looked inside myself to see what was there, to discover why I had been operating this ministry in the name of God, in the name of mission work, or parachurch ministry or some other word that merely means we can't chase the demons from ourselves so we'll play Jesus to the lepers in other people's psyches. It's just another form of escapism. Ministry is full of folks bent on this mission. Usually they crash and seek escape in porn, adultery, or you fill in the blank. Me? The words on this page. I think. Maybe. I love to build them, stack them, scoot them around to the last paragraph. But mostly, I sit in my office here at church feeling that I'm not worthy to be in this chair behind this desk behind this closed door behind these church walls behind this face. There was a time when something on the inside screamed for accolades. I longed for the world's approval. But every time I sensed it was in my grasp, I couldn't reach it. It was like that teenager, aloof and hard to run down in a world that screams, "Here's success, grab it! A little closer now. Do you see it? Reach higher. Dig a little deeper ... ah! It jumped out the window. Start over again."

CAN'T YOU SEE WHAT I DON'T CARE TO LOOK AT?

Denial has been around a long time. It manifested itself beside a fire during the Passion Week. The rooster crowed in the third watch of

Peter's dark night of the soul, and Augustine once said, "Before God can deliver us from ourselves, we must first undeceive ourselves."

Getting out of the BED of

3. *Denial—the art of deceiving ourselves so we believe our own lies.* "'No!' Peter insisted. 'Not even if I have to die with you! I will never deny you!' And all the other disciples vowed the same" (Matthew 26:35).

Saying Too Much

The dog days of summer passed and no bill for the hotel room damage arrived in the mail. I figured they'd forgotten or lost the bill, which relieved my guilt, making it easier to attend the same conference the following year at the same hotel in Florida. (Never return to the scene of a crime.) I was okay until I stepped onto the hotel property. Then I feared hotel management would single me out in the long lunch line. "There he is. I'd recognize that nose anywhere. Get him, boys!" So I positioned my sunglasses a little lower on my nose, shrinking my snout by a good three inches. I never walked anywhere alone. I elbowed my way into the epicenter of every teenage huddle that was going my way, hiding among sweaty underarms and teen spirit.

I made it to the end of the week without anyone even mentioning the damage—not the maid, not the management, not even the teens. I fell into denial that it even happened. I pushed the horrible scene out of my mind.

On the last day, while I was herding the kids outside, trying to get them loaded on the van to go home, two of the boys in my youth group approached me with a bill. They said hotel management was looking for me. The hotel wanted me to pay the bill before I left. I opened it and read:

Dear Mr. Stofel:

The following is a bill for the damage incurred to Room 316 last summer during the youth conference. The damages and their totals are as follows:

Carpet: $400.00

Paint: $200.00

Cleaning Fee: $100.00

Maintenance fee to replace smoke alarm and cost of smoke alarm: $200.00

Total Bill: $900.00

Sincerely,
The Management

My brain did somersaults. I got everybody in the white fifteen-passenger van and pulled around to the office and got out. Then I leaned back in and ordered the two boys to get out while telling the rest to stay put. "Nobody gets out of this van!" Blank stares answered the threat. *Just try me,* my eyes threatened. *If I had to pay, then they'd pay double for their sin of getting out of the van.* I was a Pharisee willing to "travel over land and sea to win a single convert," but if one of them stepped out of that van, I was willing to "make him twice as much a son of hell."

I walked to the hotel office with the two teenage boys attached to my hips, and it was another defining moment, a moment that I thought I'd eluded. I stuck my elbows on the counter and announced I was there to pay the bill for damages. The woman looked at me as if I were out of my mind. It was clear she didn't know what I was talking about, and just before I blabbed the firecracker story again, the two teenage boys grabbed both of my arms and pulled me away from the counter, trying to convey something to me. They were laughing so hard they couldn't get it out, and every time they tried, they doubled over in hilarity. I didn't see the humor in it, and all they could say was a whispered, "Be quiet."

"What are you doing to me?" I blurted out when they'd success-fully dragged me through the front door of the hotel and back out into the humid air.

"It was us! It was us! We wrote the bill. It's a bogus bill!"

"What are you talking about?" I said with a flushed face.

"We made up the bill."

"How did you get access to a computer?" I shot back.

"We made it before we left home."

So they had conspired to take me out. It was a premeditated prank, and I started slapping them on the shoulders, pushing them away with "How could you do this to me?" phrases. After I calmed down and quit pacing the curb in front of the hotel, I walked out to the van to find teens laughing and pointing at me through the window.

I found out later that the reason hotel management hadn't sent me a bill was because the bill had been taken care of—not by the church, but by a scheduled renovation. Hotel management had planned, unknown to me, to remodel the battle-scarred room, even while I was burning a hole in the carpet. Behind the scenes of my own destruction, the plan to renovate was already in place. And so it is with God. "God demonstrates his own love for us in this: While we were still sinners, Christ died for us" (Romans 5:8).

HIGHWAYS WILL GET
YOU ONLY SO FAR

Count on Personal Relationships to Carry You Further

I TRAVELED TO BOSTON in a rented mammoth blue Cadillac with a bald man singing hymns. We were after some dream, some completely idiotic theory that our lives were getting ready to change. He'd shove in a tape of hymns, grip the steering wheel with both hands, throw back his head, and belt out an anthem while driving through the Pocono Mountains.

... But before any of this, that summer, the bald guy and I met like two deranged prophets colliding in a field. I was Elisha and he was Elijah seeking God in the whirlwind. He walked the streets of his neighborhood, and he prayed agonizing prayers to a God who seemed deaf. He felt cornered and alone. I was a painter then. My hair was long, my body skinny. Angular bones protruded from a shirt speckled with paint, only a few years away from a life of drugs. God had delivered me, and I was trying to figure out how to pray. So I hung out with some veteran prayer warriors and listened. But what I heard was not so much from them as it was from God. I felt that God was giving me a prophetic word for someone who doubted his love and guidance. I didn't say anything to my mentors. They would've doubted me out of it, maybe. Or maybe I was scared to say that I'd actually heard God speak. It can be embarrassing for a former drug addict to talk about hearing God. "Okay, what have you been smoking?" my friends would be sure to ask. So I kept it to myself.

Every Friday after prayer at one of the businessmen's office, we would go get a cup of coffee at a fast-food joint behind the boot store in Brentwood, Tennessee. Here's the setting and characters:

Setting: Six businessmen and one painter sitting around a table in a fast-food restaurant, each holding a coffee cup in his palms while the steam encircles the rim of the cup. Three tables over sits a lone bald man with coffee and a biscuit. There are others, some standing at the counter ordering, others at their tables eating and reading the morning paper or talking.

My point of view: Six businessmen talking about the latest biblical insight, and off to the left, a lone bald man peeling back the wrapper on his biscuit like a surgeon revealing cancer, and a quick slap of butter between the two halves, and then a bite. He looked lonely and stressed. His veins joggled in his temple as he chewed.

Bald Man's point of view: Six businessmen and a drug addict that these men are seemingly trying to rehabilitate. A charity case, no doubt. Pro bono work.

This was the setting every Friday at the restaurant behind the huge boot sign.

I'd been watching the lone man for weeks. I felt he was the recipient of my word from God. But I didn't know how to deliver it. I was new at this, a rookie prayer warrior who probably had a better shot at hearing God before he got inoculated with religion. But delivery was a problem. I was shy. Not a good thing for God to give an introvert a message to deliver. High stakes and blood pressure.

One Friday I watched the bald man leave the restaurant. A small dog was scratching at the side window of his two-seater Mercedes. Not good. Means money! Maybe. That's great. He'll think I'm after his money (especially after I found out he thought I was a charity project for the businessmen—pro bono or something.)

The next Friday, same scene as the prior week. I saw him get up with that small piece of biscuit he was saving for his dog. He approached our table. I got tense. I knew it was now or never. I let him walk by. I chastised myself for a week. Why couldn't I tell a man I had a word from God for him?

The following week I decided to end the charade. When he got up to exit, I stepped in front of him and stuck out my bony hand with dried paint beneath my nails and said, "I'm Robert Stofel." (I gave him my formal name, figuring it was a formal introduction.)

"Roy Clarke, Rob," he said in a deep Bostonian accent.

I tried some humor in the awkward moment. "You're not the singer guy?"

"No, I can't play a guitar."

Nervous laughs.

He asked, "Are you guys believers?"

"Yes, why don't you join us at our table?"

"I think I will," he said.

Ah! Did it! There he sat with six businessmen and a lone painter with long hair; the message from God was far from me in that moment. I knew he was the recipient of what God wanted to say, but how do you deliver such a message? I didn't tell him about the crazy word from God. I wasn't sure. I was apprehensive, thinking maybe it was a message from my own twisted mind.

When Hearing Is Seeing

Weeks elapsed. Moons waxed and waned. Mud puddles dried. Five Fridays in the history books. Every Friday he was there among us. He'd been accepted into the group, and one day he told us what he had previously thought was taking place with these six businessmen and one drug-addict–booze-drinker–painter. (Not that all painters are drunks and addicts.)

"I thought you guys were counseling this addict back to health."

The six businessmen liked the sound of it. It amused them to think of themselves in that role.

Then one morning, Roy drove his Mercedes two-seater over to an apartment complex where I was painting. I had a small business painting apartments. After people moved out, I painted the apartment before the next occupant moved in. I was trying to work my way through Middle Tennessee State University at the ripe old age of 26. I was married with two young daughters, eking out a living.

Roy walked into the empty apartment that contained only a paint sprayer sitting in the middle of the living room floor on a drop cloth with the sprayer tube resting inside a five-gallon bucket of paint. We talked awhile leaning up against the kitchen counters where my tools were spread out for easy access.

I said, "You know, I never told you why I introduced myself to you that morning. Now don't laugh at me, because I'm new at this stuff of hearing God, but I felt God had given me a message for you."

"Really," he said. "What's the message?"

I hesitated; then, "I hear your prayers and I care for you."

I thought he'd smile and say, "That's interesting," then move on to some other topic or conversation piece that involved current events. So when his eyes welled with emotion, and he said, "The morning you introduced yourself to me, I was walking my block for exercise, telling God he must not be listening, that he must not care, that I didn't even have a friend in this town. Then you introduced yourself to me."

Slight smiles were exchanged. Then silence. I didn't know what to say because I never expected to encounter God like this. But I knew something else was happening. I was learning more than prayer. I was experiencing community. I discovered how people can carry us further on our jouneys.

Dietrich Bonhoeffer believed, "The physical presence of other Christians is a source of incomparable joy and strength to the believer. ... It is grace, nothing but grace, that we are allowed to live in community with Christian brethren."[1]

ALLOWING OTHERS TO BECOME

Whenever we open our lives to other people, there's the risk of control. Control freaks can prey on those who appear weak. Be careful here. Become wise. Here's a good question to ask when you're allowing others to encourage you and admonish you: "Is this person dominating me, regulating my actions, and coercing me to do things that make me feel uncomfortable?"

If yes, then it's human control and not spiritual love. We have to be able to discern manipulation from true fellowship. "Spiritual love recognizes the true image of the other person which he has received from Jesus Christ."[2]

Relationships carry us further when we find someone who can look beyond what we are to find what we might become. Jesus looked beyond the clay feet of Peter and called him "The Rock," even though he denied Jesus three times.

WHY SHOULD I ATTEND CHURCH

Often I get asked if a perosn has to attend church to be a Christian, and I tell them that they can worship God at home, in a car, or in the break room at work. Worship can happen anywhere, but the existence of a church is unique in the fact that God has called believers to meet together. When we come together as a church assembly, it allows us to do what Hebrews 10:24–25 speaks of:

> And let us consider one another in order to stir up love and good works, not forsaking the assembling of ourselves

together, as is the manner of some, but exhorting one another,
and so much the more as you see the Day approaching.

Assembling ourselves together as a church body helps stir up love
and good works. Meeting together gives us an opportunity to exhort
one another, to encourage one another. It gives love an opportunity to
work in other believers' lives, not as an organization that owns brick
and mortar, but as other believers who will listen and care and teach
and admonish. "We work together as partners who belong to God. You
are God's field, God's building—not our's" (1 Corinthians 3:9 NKJV).
We are the church God is building. He isn't building a brick-and-mortar
structure, but a living temple that resides in every belieer, making the
church a place where we can "dwell together in church fellowship, and
in that fellowship, one essential matter is unity."³

  D. L. Moody once called on a leading citizen in Chicago in order to
persuade him to accept Christ. They were seated in the man's parlor. It
was winter and coal was burning in the fireplace. The man stated that
he could be a Christian and not attend church. He believed he could be
as good of a Christian outside the church as he could in it.

  Moody said nothing, but stepped to the fireplace, took the tongs,
picked a blazing coal from the fire and set it off by itself. In silence the
two watched it smolder and go out. "I see," said the man.⁴

A FREE-FLOATING ENCOURAGEMENT

A few months later, while Roy and I were munching on biscuits in the
fast-food restaurant on a day other than Friday, he handed me a
Gordon-Conwell Theological Seminary catalog and said, "Have you
ever considered going to seminary?"

  "Never."

  "I think you should consider going."

  "Me?" I asked, pointing to my chest.

  "Rob, God has his hand on you, and you need to think seriously about this. The school is in Boston, and you'd have to move. It would be a giant step."

I took the catalog and flipped through the pages, glancing up at every new page to see if he was kidding. I'd never lived out of the state of Tennessee. I'd visited the panhandle of Florida. I'd seen Rock City, but I'd never been to Boston, and he wanted me to move there, to go to school there!

Roy was one of the first people to nudge me toward full-time ministry. I was a part-time youth pastor and a full-time painter, finishing my senior year at Middle Tennessee State University. It was a big challenge, and that fall he rented a mammoth blue Cadillac, and we traveled up I-81 to Boston.

On the way to Boston, Roy taught me how to say Massachusetts. I pronounced it with a Tennessee twang: Mass-a-two-setts.

"Listen. It's Mass-a-chew ... chew-setts," he'd say, snapping his jaw.

And I'd try again, unable to get the "chew" where it needed to be, while the Cadillac floated over hills and barreled through valleys, leading me away from home and safety.

When we arrived in Boston, we got directions to the seminary. It was snuggled in a community north of Boston called South Hamilton, and Roy shouted when we passed Gordon-Conwell's sign leading to the campus. "We're here, kid!"

He likes to call me "kid." It's his word of affection. I know I'm the son he never had and that I'd stumbled into one of his dreams, but I knew that out of his dream, mine would begin.

We parked the Cadillac in front of an old church, got out, and looked in every direction, taking in the scenery as if we were on the verge of buying the place. Inside the administrative building, I introduced myself with a long Southern drawl. They were expecting me, and they looked up from their desks and smiled and mused and listened intently to this Southern aberration.

I filled out the application while Roy sat fidgety beside me. Then we nervously awaited their decision and walked the massive hallway. Thirty minutes later the jury was back. We clambered into the admissions office and both took seats as if we'd been called to the principal's office as third-graders. I was accepted!

I never thought I could become a seminary student, Elisha probably felt he'd be strapped to that plow forever, and David never set out to be king. He was a loner in the hills of a nomad land when a personal relationship ushered him into the presence of King Saul. Some servant overheard the discussion about getting a musician for the melancholic King Saul and he spoke up. "One of the servants said to Saul, 'The son of Jesse is a talented harp player. Not only that; he is brave and strong and has good judgment. ... and the LORD is with him.' So Saul sent messengers to Jesse to say, 'Send me your son David, the shepherd'" (1 Samuel 16:18–19).

David played the harp like Muddy Waters played the blues. David's music was anointed and deeply moving. But Saul's blues would've never been chased away if it hadn't been for a servant who knew David. Maybe the servant traveled over the hills and through the valleys to where David protected the sheep to hear his friend play the harp. Maybe he told David that "one of these days, you'll hit it big!" We don't know, but we do know that it was a personal relationship that carried David further, which is not to diminish God's providence in his life. Sometimes God uses people to get us where we need to be.

I had no idea that a mere introduction to a man in a fast-food restaurant was going to carry both of us further than our current roads were taking us. He was trying to find a reason for his troubles, and I was looking for a destiny. I didn't know telling someone that God hears his prayers and cares for him would change my life. I wasn't one who went around poking my nose into people's lives on a regular basis. I can't explain to you how I heard God's voice. I can only tell you that discovering it changed my life and Roy Clarke's life.

Roy had been a CEO of a company. He'd made his fortune and lost it. Now he was a middle-aged man running scared in his neighborhood, alone and wondering if God could hear him.

Roy and I were so far apart only a humorous God could have caused us to collide with one another in a fast-food restaurant. Only a God of compassion would have placed a message for someone with a boy who no more looked like a saint or the conduit for the comforting words of God than he did a goodwill project for successful businessmen in their suits and ties.

I'm not trying to make you believe I received this gift of grace on my own merit. I didn't. It was purely a moment when God put two people together to get them further down the road. That's all. That's the kind of God we serve.

Roy started attending the church where I was a member. There he met a man who became another conduit to get Roy further than his lonely road was taking him, because this man was a VP in a publishing company. The two of them discovered a mutual love for Charles Haddon Spurgeon, a preacher who filled his six-thousand-seat church in London consistently from 1861 until his death in 1892, and who today still influences the hearts and minds of those who read his works. Roy was a scholar of Spurgeon's works, a believer in what Spurgeon's words could do to direct and comfort us on our journeys. When the VP discovered Roy's scholarly magnitude concerning Spurgeon's works, he put together the idea of Roy's editing and updating Spurgeon's classic *Morning and Evening* devotional. Then Roy went on to update Spurgeon's *Treasury of David*.

When God wants to get you further than your road is taking you, he will mostly use people who don't have a ghost of a clue about what is getting ready to happen, because if they did, they'd let their pride destroy what God had in mind. Ego kills the spontaneity of God's grace.

There's a place in our journeys where God uses people because he knows that the journey can get lonely and confusing. Says Bonhoeffer,

"So between the death of Christ and the Last Day it is only a gracious anticipation of the last things that Christians are privileged to live in visible fellowship with other Christians."[5]

This is the joy I found. The "gracious anticipation" that even in our mismanagement, even in our unforgiveness, even in our overburdened souls, even in the place where you feel that not even God could reach and touch, there's a fellowship "between the death of Christ and the Last Day." It's called Christian community. Community points us to the larger purpose, where we say with the psalmist, "How wonderful it is, how pleasant, when brothers live together in harmony!" (Psalm 133:1). And unity is one of the sweetest things we have in the terrible ticking between the death of Christ and the Last Day. In community we discover how fellowship can take us further than our sad roads can carry us.

DETOURS, SHORTCUTS, AND ROADBLOCKS

When Things Don't Work out the Way You Planned

I SHATTERED THE ROMANCE on a weekend getaway. Jill and I had accepted an invitation to stay in a friend's vacation home, just the two of us. It was our tenth wedding anniversary and first weekend getaway in over a year. Snow started falling early that morning and stopped midafternoon, turning the streets into slippery white slopes, and the more it snowed, the more the wiper blades stuck to our Isuzu Rodeo's frozen windshield.

The gravel road to the log cabin in the boondocks was covered with snow that looked like white frosting spread over a cheese grater. It was a perfect winter wonderland, the way the snow perched on fence posts and clung to power lines, the way everything was frozen in its form as if Nature were playing a game of freeze tag. We, however, had escaped Nature's icy tap and had high hopes this weekend might rekindle our romance.

I pulled up to the cattle gate entrance and unlocked the padlock. Jill jumped over into the driver's seat and gassed the Rodeo through the gate while I securely relocked it. Then I jumped into the waiting passenger seat and we fishtailed to the cabin underneath snow-filled trees. We were locked inside a paradise and no one would be able to disturb us.

Both of us abandoned the car to get a preliminary look at the cabin. We were anxious to see if it matched what we'd imagined. Firewood was stacked on the porch beside the door that had two vertical windows on each side. I unlocked the door with anticipation, walked in, and placed the keys on a table beside the door. I gazed up to a loft, and then down at a massive bear rug spread out on the floor in front of a stone fireplace. The walls were decorated with Ponderosa flare, and we looked at each other and smiled the nobody-for-miles-around smile.

Jill broke the smiling and said, "Let's unload the car."

We got our duffel bags and hustled back to the cabin, as if it might change its mind and refuse us entry. I grabbed the doorknob, but it wouldn't turn. It was locked. No problem. I reached into my pocket for the keys. No keys. I peered through the vertical window by the door to find them on the table.

Jill asked, "What's wrong? ... Don't tell me you left the keys in the cabin."

"I didn't know the door locked automatically."

"This is great, just great," she said, dropping her duffel bag beside the door. "What were you thinking?"

I knew I'd better not even attempt to answer. I didn't see a solution in sight, so I listened attentively to her desperation. John Gray would have been proud of me. I didn't try to fix her. I left her on Venus and wished I were on Mars.

She tried again through quivering lips, "So, what are we going to do?"

I knew her heart was broken. I knew she'd been looking forward to this trip for some time. She always gets a little giddy when we take a vacation, and now it was ruined.

"Maybe they have a spare key out here somewhere," I said fishing around in every crevice and long-abandoned spider web. No key. And as minutes turned into an hour, it was evident that we were stranded in the middle of nowhere, about to become a "Dateline" survivor story.

THE OPTIONS

After Jill threw a handful of snow at me, we started to weigh our options.

1. Call someone. (We couldn't because the phone was in the house, and I was too cheap to buy a cell phone.)

2. Drive home. (I'd locked the gate.)

3. Walk to a friendly farmer's house. (We saw no friendly lights and knew no one; besides, these days the friendly farmer is a myth. Plus, you could wind up like that man in the movie *Misery*—snowed in and tortured by a crazy person.)

4. Break in and enter. (It would mean no more invitations to the cabin.)

5. Flip a coin to see who walks back to civilization with only a slice of moon to guide, risking frostbite. (We both liked our toes; besides, I'd lose either way.)

LAST-DITCH EFFORT

We stood around the porch, taking up new positions. We turned at a dozen paces, for love is a duel, and looked at each other. She'd move, and then I'd make a defensive move. She walked to the window by the door that leaked the light of what used to be a romantic hideaway, and this is when it came to me. I knew what needed to be done. I went to the car and got my tire tool.

"Move back. I'm going to break the window," I said, choosing option four.

It took three blows. Then I reached in and unlocked the door. We were in! But the weekend wasn't the same after that. Our getaway became a crime scene, and not only was the window shattered, so was the romance.

MILES AND MILES

Sometimes life is like a getaway weekend gone bad. Life starts out with hoopla and ends in shattered pieces, and when it doesn't turn out as we planned, we wind up choosing the wrong option. We choose despair instead of hope. We choose holding a grudge instead of forgiving. We choose quitting over persevering. Sometimes we make the wrong choice and focus on one solution when there are many ways to overcome.

In the book *Woulda, Coulda, Shoulda*, the authors refer to a certain scene in the movie *Blazing Saddles*, in which the good guys are being chased by the bad guys through the desert. "The good guys have to figure out a way to slow the bad guys down. And what do they do? They set up a tollbooth."[1]

Anyone who comes across a tollbooth in the desert needs only to go around it, but the bad guys didn't. They galloped their horses to the tollbooth and yanked back on the reins just shy of the gate as a dust cloud pushed in behind them. Then an argument started about who had nickels, and then, ultimately, who would go back to town and retrieve more nickels. Freeman and DeWolf write, "They are so focused on the *barrier* that the tollbooth presents that they don't see all those miles and miles of open desert on either side of it."[2]

Maybe you've been hurt by divorce and you've been so focused on the failure it suggests that you haven't allowed yourself to heal. Maybe your dreams of being married have come to a halt just shy of a looming tollbooth and you don't have the energy to go back to town to get nickels. See this for what it is—a tollbooth in the desert. I know it is overwhelming, but the tollbooth, exists as a stumbling block because you feel as if you must pay, that you must punish yourself the way you think God would. You are trying to pay the toll on your own. Look beyond it to discover miles and miles of other options.

The one thing we don't have in times of brokenness is clarity. We second-guess every decision. Why? Because we've been wrong on a massive scale, so how can we be sure we'll make a wise decision in the

future? See the tollbooth for what it is and move past it. Yes, ask forgiveness. By all means, make it right between you and God. But don't
stay at the tollbooth and punish yourself or keep traveling to town to
get more nickels. There aren't enough nickels. There's only One who
can pay such a high price. He paid the toll at the Cross. So forgive yourself. You made a mistake. But life is not over. You serve the God of a
broken plan who instructs us to "'come now, and let us reason
together,' says the Lord, 'Though your sins are like scarlet, they shall be
as white as snow'" (Isaiah 1:18 NKJV). When we talk with God and ask
forgiveness, he takes the leftovers of a broken plan and points out miles
and miles surrounding our situation.

HANDLING LIFE'S SECOND BESTS

Harry Emerson Fosdick calls the leftovers of a broken plan "handling
life's second bests." Fosdick believes few people "have a chance to live
their lives on the basis of their first choice. We all have to live upon the
basis of our second and third choices."[3]

Paul's second missionary journey was etched with the leftovers of
a broken plan. When he tried to take the Gospel into Asia, he met
tough resistance from a source he'd never considered. "They headed
for the province of Bithynia, but again the Spirit of Jesus did not let
them go. So instead, they went on through Mysia to the city of Troas"
(Acts 16:7–8). It's strange that Jesus would thwart a missionary plan,
unless we knew that the tollbooth, the blockade, was leading Paul
another way, a way that would take Christianity into miles and miles
of new territory.

A lot of us find ourselves in situations where the road to a certain
future is blocked. "Life has not turned out the way I planned," we say.
But God may see it as the most significant part of our stories, because
this is when we turn our stories over to him. We *all* have to get to the
point where we accept our Troas and release our Bithynia; not that following God got easier for Paul, for it didn't. It only got more adventurous.

SPLINTERED THOUGHTS

After my tire tool splintered the glass, I stuck my hand through the broken window and unlocked the door. Glass crunched under the shoes of option four. We had to live with the remains of a broken plan. Our romance was cold as the wind that screeched through the broken window, which I covered with trash bags from the kitchen pantry. The awareness of this wound made us feel as if we had to fix something. We found ourselves constantly staring at the window. It became the tollbooth that we couldn't get past, the tollbooth that dogged us with self-punishment. *How could you do this? You're worthless. You're broken.*

Tollbooths shouldn't be our first contact with the world. When we seek God first, instead of trying to correct or get through some tollbooth that has belittled us, we release ourselves from the shame, forgiving ourselves as Christ has forgiven us, and this is when we see miles and miles around the tollbooth. Not that the tollbooth has been erased from our emotions, but we learn that we can never pay the price for our sin. We repent and follow God, but the miles and miles will still have other tollbooths that must be defeated. James Thurber put it this way: "All persons must learn before they die, what they're running from and what they're running to, and why." To learn this before we die is to understand our tollbooths; if not, we travel a life of familiar emotional pain.

FAMILIAR EMOTIONAL PAIN

Life is too short to remain in a cycle, and the way to spot the emotional terrain of pain is by reviewing our prayers. If we discover that our prayers are fixated on past, then emotional pain may be at the heart of our prayers. Sometimes we pray more for release than we do for change. When prayer for release becomes our sole contact with God, then we stunt our spiritual growth. We never get past the tollbooth.

Are you caught in a loop between the tollbooth and going back to town for more nickels? This loop is our attempt at alleviating emotional pain. When we fixate on a problem instead of moving beyond the toll-booth, each loop, each return trip from the supply of nickels to the toll-booth, compounds emotional pain, causing us to feel overwhelmed. When weighed down with emotional pain, we reach for our own remedy, such as drugs, alcohol, or thrill-seeking. These things won't move us beyond the tollbooth. Pray for change more than you do for release.

Killing the View of an Ox's Rump

Elisha broke up his wooden plow and made a fire to roast his oxen. He was ready to burn his past. "Elisha then returned to his oxen, killed them, and used the wood from the plow to build a fire to roast their flesh. He passed around the meat to the other plowmen, and they all ate. Then he went with Elijah as his assistant" (1 Kings 19:21).

He broke apart or killed the tools of his trade. There would be no retreat. He wanted to close this chapter of his life. The way to put the past behind you is by following Elisha's process: (1) kill the beasts, and (2) destroy the plow.

Maybe you need to burn a few plows. Only you can pry your hands free from the past. There is no magic potion. The only way out is to kill the ox—that one thing that holds you in bondage. Without the life of the ox there'd be no plowing. So stop feeding him. Because if the ox can get one morsel of your thought life, then he'll be back for more, and this time he'll plow up your confidence, your self-worth, your psychological well-being. So kill the ox! Destroy the plow!

Elisha had longed for this moment. He'd stared at the rumps of oxen so long that he didn't know there was a sunset. You and I both know people who, when handed a sunset, will go back to the view of an ox's rump. Why such behavior? They feel it's their duty to make it past the tollbooths in their own strength, while others simply can't face the pain of change, so the busyness of traveling the loop becomes another form of denial.

When we put to death old emotions, we'll feel detached—and that's normal. No one does all of this in one day. You can bet Elisha had days when his thoughts drifted back to the smell and the comfort of having only one responsibility—plowing. This is the deception of the past—*it used to be so easy.*

Elisha safeguarded himself against the possibility of quitting. He knew, at the first sign of suffering, that his mind would drift back to where it was safe, but when you have nowhere to go but forward, then you learn to persevere. When you face your past, disassemble it, and close the curtain, you'll move from the present into the future. Elisha was smart enough to know that life would never be the same, and to go back and recreate a past life would be dangerous to the future. So it is with us. Kill the ox and get on with the rest of your life. Put the past where it belongs—in the past. The God of the broken plan can bring out of our bleak, frightening experiences the redemptive act that works beneath the layer of suffering. Trials turn into divine moments when God approaches and causes all things to work together for good. Learning how to change our view from hopelessness to faith depends on how we view the tollbooth.

Holy Doldrums

Self-pity is just another means of control. If I can get you to feel sorry for me, then you will help me get another drink. You will allow me to stay in my distant country, away from God's dreams for my life, and this is called enabling. Self-pity knows how to lob guilt into every relationship. "Can't you see I'm a victim?" self-pity asks. And the only way to deal with self-pity is to confront it.

Paul's plans may have changed, but he remained faithful to his missionary endeavors. He could've crawled in bed that night with the remains of a broken dream on his brow. He could've blamed God for thwarting his plans. Paul could've driven that stake deep into his faith and felt as if he'd somehow missed God. He could've shut down the missionary journey and headed home to make new tents on a dreary day—and even though he didn't, sometimes we do. We build our lives upon wishes and dreams that hardly ever come true. "I want to live in a castle at the beach and have a bank account full of money." It happens for some people. We know this much is true, but what if it doesn't happen for us? Will we still love God for who he is, or are we into God for what we can get out of him? The one true and holy thing in our lives is the moment we start clinging to God for who he is instead of for what he can give us.

Wherever we spend our nickels the most—trying to correct a wrong that never changes or releases you from its guilt—is reoccurring negative emotional terrain. Is there a looming pain that you keep returning to, wishing you had one more nickel that would get you past it? Do you long for one more shot at some lost love or one more chance at a profession you failed miserably at, or a marriage that has all but died except in your own heart? Emotional tollbooths make you pay and pay and pay and pay, until your strength is zapped and your hope is crushed under the weight of not being able to get past emotional pain.

THE ETERNAL PURPOSE

Paul's focus was on the eternal purpose. He knew how to get past the detours and the roadblocks of tollbooths. In every circumstance on Paul's second missionary journey, he experienced highs and lows. At one minute, he was baptizing Lydia's household, the next he was arrested and thrown in jail at Philippi for casting a demon out of a slave girl who had a spirit of divination. Then, while Paul and Silas were praising God, the shackles on their feet broke and the prison door swung open, freeing them from their bondage. They weren't down in the mouth. They were singing. They worshiped! They refused to allow their circumstances to shape the character of their faith.

The eternal purpose was Paul's focus when things strayed from the plans he'd made.

CONFESSIONS OF A BROKEN WEEKEND GETAWAY

It took me over a day to call the friend who owned the cabin. I had conversations in my head about how he would yell at me and accuse me of being irresponsible. But I knew I had to return to the terrain of the broken window to put it behind me. And there are times when we have to make wrongs right. But other times, we need to move on and see the miles and miles for what they are—God's redemption, God's way of redirecting our steps, and this is what I encountered with my friend. He was great. He didn't yell or sigh or act as if he was going to die. He forgave me. He released me from the bondage of guilt.

Maybe you need to return to some area of your life where an injury, an offense, a mistake, an injustice took place. Free yourself from it once and for all. Then look on each side of the tollbooth. Do you see the miles and miles?

WHEN YOU FEEL LIFE
SLIP-SLIDING AWAY

Dealing with the Fear Beneath Our Circumstances

TO MAKE THE TEAM you had to face Big Russ Pace, who wasn't your everyday, run-of-the-mill, twelve-year-old pitcher. He was Orel Hershiser, Greg Maddux, and David Wells all rolled into one, and he loved to send kids home to their mommies. Because if a kid had any chance at making Toby's Chicken Kitchen—a Little League baseball team—then he'd have to swing at Big Russ Pace's Scud missiles.

I was twelve and weighed every bit of seventy pounds soaking wet, but I was determined to try out. I oiled the glove. Daddy lifted the corner of the refrigerator and placed it underneath. It cured like a smoked ham while I slept. Then I rose early and whacked a baseball into its tenderness for hours, abusing it, making it conform to my hand. And in the afternoon, I practiced my swing. I'd hit the ball across the street, which was a home run in our neighborhood. We had everything mapped out. We knew the boundaries. We knew when to back up or move in closer, according to who stepped up to bat at our makeshift home plate, which doubled as a T-shirt. I had no problem facing down my foes in the neighborhood, but Big Russ Pace was the sum of all fears.

Swing, Batter Batter, Swing

Big Russ Pace stood on the mound like a beast out of the sea of apocalyptic horror. He'd stare you down as you approached the plate. I never looked his way. I scratched the dirt with my new cleats, pounded the plate, and adjusted my batting helmet, fighting hard to keep it balanced on my head, which made me look like a bobble-head doll in the back windshield of a car. I couldn't see out from under it. But who cared? Closed eyes were the only way to face Big Russ Pace.

I could hear my father in the bleachers, "All right, let's go. Hit the ball. Stand in there. Don't be a sissy."

The coach shouted, "Get the bat off of your shoulders. ... Come on now, you can do it."

The rest of the team sat in the dugout blowing bubbles with the gum that came packaged as a pouch of chewing tobacco. (We pretended it was Red Man.) They worked their jaws and said nothing, knowing I wouldn't be able to hit the ball. They'd seen me the day before and the day before that, and now it was the last day to be cut.

Big Russ Pace leaned forward, putting his hands behind him, rocked back, and launched from his left arm a fireball. I closed my eyes. Then I peeped to discover the ball headed for my head. But right before the ball took my head off, it curved and popped the catcher's glove—strike! I gave the coach a quick glance and discovered I was outside the batter's box.

Jeering started. It was outright disdain. No one runs from the batter's box, but when Russ Pace climbed the mound, he became larger than every little boy's dream of making a Little League baseball team. And you guessed it. I got cut from the team. The coach asked me to be batboy, so unable to face Big Russ Pace, I settled for holding his bat and glove. I was unable to face fear and defeat it.

The Elimination of All-or-Nothing

Wouldn't it be great if we could eliminate all the Big Russ Paces in our lives, eradicating the sum of all our fears? Would we go for our dream job? Would we make a commitment and get married? Would we have another child? Would we follow God?

The way into the future is to face our fears and defeat them. We have to let go of fear to discover contentment, and the way fear works has to do with all-or-nothing thinking, which is the belief that if we don't have a perfect situation in our life at this moment, then we have nothing. All-or-nothing thinking causes our emotions to be heightened for no reason and produces panic—the extreme belief that we're in danger of losing all.[1]

All-or-nothing thinking is what Jesus spoke against when he said, "Can all your worries add a single moment to your life? Of course not! And if worry can't do little things like that, what's the use of worrying over bigger things?" (Luke 12:25-26).

I believe that's why Jesus put so much emphasis on two little words, "Fear not." He knew we'd struggle with fear. So ask yourself, "Is the fear I'm feeling good fear or bad fear?" And when I say, "good or bad," I mean, is it unrealistic fretting? Because sometimes fear can be damaging, and at other times it's good. There's a good side to fear that keeps us from jumping off tall buildings or driving our car over a cliff. Ernest Ligon says, "Fear must not be confused with caution."[2]

It's this dual role of fear that makes it confusing.

If we can't attach concrete evidence to our thoughts of fear or anger or envy, then it's worrying about nothing. No one can see what tomorrow will bring, but we burden ourselves and waste time on unrealities. The ailment of humanity is unrealistic fretting. Half of the circumstances that we worry about will never happen. They're a figment of our imagination. There's a way to test it. As someone has said, "Start a journal. List all of the things you're worried about. Then wait a month and reread them to find out which ones became a reality." My bet is nine out of ten will never happen. You should test things before you fret over them. Ask "Is the fear I'm feeling really true?" True fear is good.

Bad fear is only worrying over unrealities. We proceed with caution, but we never push forward in fear.

Ernest Ligon writes, "Fear, then, is simply an expression of conflict. When conflicts occur, a number of things result. In the first place, these conflicts always weaken personality because mental drives neutralize one another instead of combining their forces toward one end."[3]

This is what happened to me when I stood before Big Russ Pace at the plate; I simultaneously closed my eyes, ducked, lowered my bat, got weak in the knees, and ran out of the batter's box. Fear made all of these motor expressions collide in the process of expression, "and the result is a state of discoordination."[4]

Fear can render us helpless, and this is the danger when we interpret the world with a lens of all-or-nothing thinking. Once our mind is taken over by fear, we fall into a state of immobilization, the way the army of Israel did when faced by Goliath. "We will settle this dispute in single combat!" he taunted. "If your man is able to kill me, then we will be your slaves. But if I kill him, you will be our slaves! I defy the armies of Israel! Send me a man who will fight with me!" When Saul and the Israelites heard this, they were terrified and deeply shaken" (I Samuel 17:8–11). This depicts "beautifully the effect of this emotion [fear] both upon motor behavior and upon mental mechanics."[5]

Notice that the Israelites were "terrified and deeply shaken." They were affected physically. They quaked in their shoes the way I quaked in my cleats. When Goliath stepped forward ranting and raving about how he'd bust the head of anybody who dared to combat him, he was just another thug with a rap single shooting up the charts. Sure, he was tall and wider than an area code. He stood nine feet tall and had a mouth the size of Montana. He was a precursor of the eighties with his bronze leggings and Dr. Scholl's inserts in his Red Wing boots. He was the father of propaganda that was handed down to Saddam Hussein, and every morning and every evening he hurled grenades of distortion into the Israelite camp, immobilizing them. "I defy the armies of Israel," he'd shout.

The Israelites feared even the airwaves that carried his booming voice across the valley. They hunkered in their foxholes with fear dripping into their veins. Then a ruddy, pimple-faced kid walked into the camp with a brown-bag lunch dangling from his musically conditioned fingers, and he asked the one question they feared: "Who is this pagan Philistine anyway, that he is allowed to defy the armies of the living God?" (I Samuel 17:26). David's question went through the camp like dysentery until it reached King Saul. No one was willing to answer this question because to answer it meant they had no real excuse. And when David's eldest brother, Eliab, heard the question he exploded, but David "just ignores him, as if to say, 'Hey, all I did was ask a question. Now, let's go on to the important thing. That giant out there.'"6

David moved in the face of fear. He chose five smooth stones. He was deliberate in his actions because David knew that action confronts fear. Taking steps to eradicate the source of our fears is the one true and holy thing we can do to move beyond them. The hard question we must ask ourselves is, "Why can't I execute my plans to make my dreams come true?"

Most people know where they want to go in life and how to get there, but they allow fear to immobilize them. And maybe Eliab, David's brother, mapped it out on the dirt floor of the world while stars fell out of the Israelite night. He may have picked out the daughter he'd marry, because Saul had put up a reward for the death of Goliath: "The man who kills him the king will enrich with great riches, will give him his daughter, and give his father's house exemption from taxes in Israel" (I Samuel 17:25 NKJV). Eliab was like every other soldier in the camp—dreaming of the good life that was wrapped up in Saul's reward—but fear held them all hostage.

Maybe you've mapped out the route you will take through college or researched how to get a state license in some trade, but you are still sitting in the camp of your own fear, burdened and unhappy. The world is full of Eliabs, because sometimes it's easier to be nothing and mad at the world than risk failure. Don't fall for that trick!

We have to make a break with fear if we are going to find our purpose and live the life we've always wanted. Charles Reynolds Brown writes, "Find yourself as one who has a definite responsibility which cannot be delegated to anybody else, and then fill your place to the brim."[7]

We have a place in this world. We're destined. But the limitation is us. Sometimes God cannot give us the future while we're complaining about the present. When we come to terms with where we are at the moment, even if it's not where we want to be, we give God room to create something new, and releasing our fears is part of the coming to terms with our present crisis.

On our family vacations, my brother and I would finally give up on receiving the answer to "Are we there yet?" We'd get lost in the moment, playing Old Maid or Go Fish! or counting the VW Bugs on the interstate. It got to the point where we trusted Dad. We'd settled in, comfortable with the assurance that we'd arrive at our destination.

DETACHMENT CAN BE REDISCOVERY

I felt detached holding Big Russ Pace's bat and glove. It was humbling. But I persevered. My time as batboy gave me the room to grow and learn. I not only handled their bats, I watched their moves, stayed close to their sides in the dugout, befriended Big Russ Pace, watched him warm up, even became his catcher during practice, and the next year I made Toby's Chicken Kitchen team. Then the year after that, when Big Russ Pace moved up to the school's team, I was given the opportunity of a little boy's lifetime. I was given a shot at the mound, and the way I got the opportunity to pitch in a real game came about when the coach saw me horsing around with the catcher at practice one

Thursday afternoon. He was chattering, "Come, batter batter, swing," while I wound up and put the ball in his target.

The coach walked over to me and said, "Son, how would you like to pitch?"

Now to say to a boy, "How would you like to pitch?" was equal to saying, "How would you like to go out with a cheerleader?"

Both were equal-employment opportunities, and I was never one to be overly excited about anything, so I shrugged my shoulders in a James Dean sort of way and said, "Sure, whatever I can do to help the team, Coach."

The following Tuesday night, under the lights at Jim Warner Park in Franklin, Tennessee, I was out in left field, literally, with my glove spread out on one knee and my open hand covering the other knee. Troy Green, the fastest pitcher on our team, was on the mound and had walked the last two batters when the coach approached the mound and retrieved the ball. Then he motioned for me to come to the pitcher's mound. What an exhilarating feeling to have all eyes following you to the mound, while mouths whispered, "I didn't know that Stofel boy could pitch." And one may have responded, "Well, he sure can't catch it, so maybe he can throw it."

The coach dropped the ball into my glove and said, "Do your best, son. Put them low and in the strike zone."

I turned to look at the plate, which seemed farther than I remembered, and I warmed up. Then the batter stepped up to the plate, and my first two balls were high and out of the strike zone. The third was a strike. The fourth was popped up and caught by the third baseman.

"All right! Keep it up, Stofel," the coach yelled. "Everybody get ready!"

This was when I saw their home-run leader step to the plate. I wanted to get a sudden cramp and be taken out of the game. But I stayed on the mound when everything inside me yelled, "Run!"

The batter scratched the plate with his bat. Then he put the bat high above his shoulder, dangling it behind his head as if a four-foot rat were standing before him.

I wound up my pitch, kicked high, and threw the ball into the ump's facemask. "Ball one." Again I tossed my fastball, which was probably the slowest ball in the league, and "Strike one!" He somehow missed it, and it gave me courage, and I slung the next one low and away. "Strike Two!" I couldn't believe he went for it. *I can strike him out,* I suddenly told myself.

The batter choked up on his bat and swayed back and forth; the catcher had felt my confidence and was chattering, "Come, batter batter, swing!"

I kicked high again and ... "Strike three! You're out!"

I struck him out! And the shortstop ran up and paddled me on the rump with his glove. The coach had his two fingers inside his mouth whistling. The crowd turned to one another and curled up their bottom lips in sudden belief. It was the birth of a pitcher and the death of a pitcher because I walked the next three and gave up two runs in the fifth. Then the coach retrieved me from the mound and said, "Not bad, kid. Take a break." Then he brought in another pitcher, and, for the rest of my Little League career, I was never put on the mound again.

The only way to deal with fear is to ruthlessly kick it out of your mind with two small words: "Fear not!" Because "the very hairs on your head are all numbered. So don't be afraid; you are more valuable to him than a whole flock of sparrows" (Luke 12:7).

So press on and fear not! Apply for that job you've always wanted. Go back to school and retool for another occupation. Pop the question to the one you've dated forever. Have another child. Be on the offensive. Take action! "Find yourself as one who has a definite responsibility which cannot be delegated to anybody else, and then fill your place to the brim." Fear not!

IS LIFE BEAUTIFUL?
I CAN'T EVER TELL

Take Time for the Scenic Route

MOST UNIVERSITIES HAVE AT least one famous person who once walked its halls, and Ole Miss claims one in the mailroom. William Faulkner—the famous southern American writer and Nobel Prize winner who lived in Oxford, Mississippi, until his death in 1962—worked at Ole Miss sorting mail and delivering it. It's said that he wouldn't deliver a magazine until he first read it, and we can see him propped up at the mailroom counter with chin in hand, flipping non-chalantly through someone else's magazine.

But these days, whoever is in the mailroom is efficient, because he or she was sending Blair letters faster than we could open them. The university was trying to entice her to leave home and travel to a distant country. But the image of Blair leaving home with her car packed to the dome light and the thrill of adventure in her eyes was too much for us to imagine.

Blair had narrowed her search to two universities—Alabama and Ole Miss. Her first visit was to Ole Miss. She was going to ride to Oxford, Mississippi, with a friend who was a returning student and had offered Blair a ride, a tour of the campus, and a place to stay for the weekend. So Blair instructed us to pick her up in Oxford on Monday.

I'd always wanted to tour the home of William Faulkner, so I got out the map, thinking the trip could be a double-edged sword—fraught with destiny and scenery.

No interstates exist between Decatur, Alabama, and Oxford, Mississippi. It's nothing but back roads and state highways. No neon signs pointing the way to exits that are havens for fast-food joints and truck stops, so I tried to focus on the beauty the trip might offer. I was thankful for a reason to travel to Oxford, anticipating a scenic drive through small towns on the verge of becoming Wal-Martized. I just wished it were under better circumstances.

"It will take us about three hours to get there," I yelled to Jill in the kitchen, where she was placing dirty dishes in the dishwasher.

Jill wanted to leave early. She's like that. I knew she'd watch every road sign and continually ask if I knew where I was going. It's my payback for hammering my dad with childlike destination questions as he worked out his vacation plans.

Panoramic View

After making a few wrong turns, Jill no longer trusted me. So I said, "whoever drew that road map didn't know what they were doing. Trust me. I know how to get to Oxford. Quit worrying about where we are and enjoy the scenery."

I thought we were on the right path, but I was too busy looking at every little town and wondering what life was like living in them. I was on the back road of my mind trying to catch the scenery hidden behind walls of hustle and bustle because we must not trick ourselves into believing that some day, when life slows down, we'll get around to taking the scenic route. Life can slip through our fingers while we cry, "How long? How much further before my dreams come true? How long until my circumstances change?" We miss the beauty of the journey.

Frederick Buechner writes, "There are lots of people who get into the habit of thinking of their time as not so much an end in itself, a time to be lived and loved and filled full for its own sake, but more as just a kind of way station on the road to somewhere else."[1]

I guess there's a little bit of way station in all of us. We all want to be something that we are not, or be somewhere we are not; we lose sight of where we are in the present. So ... slow down and take a back road. Stop at the scenic view. Look behind walls of hustle and bustle and discover panoramic views. Jesus alluded to this in Luke: "Consider how the lilies grow. They do not labor or spin. Yet I tell you, not even Solomon in all his splendor was dressed like one of these" (12:27 NIV). Jesus points out a scenic view and says, in essence, "Stop, look, and consider. Take the scenic route for a minute. What do you see?" Then he points out the provision locked up in this scenic view, which reminds us that we're not lone travelers. Martin Luther always had a flower on his writing desk for inspiration, allowing the botany of Christ's words to develop a sense of providence.[2]

DIRECTIONS TO THE OBVIOUS

I could tell Jill's apprehension of my navigation skills was escalating. I was ready to throw the map out the window. It had been nothing but a source of tension ever since we left Alabama. She kept it in her lap, tapped it every now and then with her delicate fingers, then finally shut it after she saw a sign pointing to University Avenue and downtown Oxford.

I said, "We're here, baby!"

She said, "You need to stop at this Exxon station and ask them where the university is."

"What for? We're headed for University Avenue and downtown Oxford. We can't get lost."

"I still think you should stop."

I wanted the trip to unfold without figuring out the complete travel plan. I wanted the scenic route, which might frustrate others at times, but the benefits far outweighed any time lost circling downtown.

I pulled into the Exxon station on the corner of South Lamar and

University Avenue. We pushed through the door to find a man behind the counter talking on a white phone. He had the cord stretched across the space behind the counter and was making casual conversation with somebody. A maintenance man was standing on a ladder. He had his hand on a wire in the tiled ceiling as if it were a snake he was beating back. He never looked down. We sluggishly shuffled over to the bathroom to give the man time to finish his conversation. I needed directions to the university from University Avenue, so I knew I wasn't high on his priority list. Oh, it would've been different if we were buying a case of Coke, a couple bags of chips, and a can of Vienna sausages, but no, we were lost on University Avenue, and we only wanted directions and the use of his bathroom.

Jill nodded toward the counter, as if to say, "Let's go, boy. Get yourself over there and do some asking. Get the show on the road."

She left me standing there. I watched her get back inside the Civic. She checked her makeup in the visor mirror. I was the only customer in the store, if you want to call me a customer. Then it hit me. It would be a lot more casual to buy something, then pop the question. *I'll pull my money out, hand it to him, and ask for directions. I've got myself a plan!* I headed out to make it happen.

On my way to the big coolers lining the back wall, I checked my wallet—credit card receipts, deposit slips, and ATM withdrawal slips were all I found. I fished in my pocket for some change. Chapstick, keys, and ninety-five cents. Ugh! I knew it'd be hard to buy a drink for that. I gazed at the different brands, looking at the prices labeled below the racks. Then it happened. I found an RC Cola for sixty-nine cents, grabbed it, and made my way to the counter. The man tried to get off the phone. He dropped those subtle little hints, but whoever was on the other end kept giving last-minute details. I stood by patiently. He glanced at me. Finally, he hung up and rang me up.

"It'll be seventy-four cents," he said.

I handed him three quarters and asked the dreaded question, "Do you know how to get to the university?"

He said, "Go straight through the light." He pointed out the window beyond the gas pumps. Then he added, "Where are you going?"

Now I have to tell you it was a tricky question, especially after he told me how to get to where I was going. I was taken confused. I felt sweat forming a layer between my hand and the RC Cola bottle. It was as if he was making sure I'd listened, and to prove it, he wanted me to give back the directions—a travel pop quiz. I didn't like his loaded question. I glanced out the window to the parked Civic, wishing Jill would wave me out. She just stared back at me. So I panicked, bent my knees, and said a dumb thing. "I'm going to the University of Mississippi."

He was nice, congenial. He wasn't a jerk about it at all. No, he was a Southern gentleman and said, "Which department are you going to at the university?"

"Oh! I'm going to Admissions."

He pointed out the window beyond the gas pumps again, and said, "Go straight until you see the Grove. Once you see the Grove, you'll need to take a left, and the student center will be on your right."

That was Southern hospitality, so I thanked the man and walked back to the Civic. Jill was proud of me—I could tell. She was sitting in the passenger's seat, smiling with her sunglasses on, sunglasses she'd been pushing up on her little pug nose ever since we left Alabama.

How Youth Is Wasted

We found the Grove. We located Blair, and we got out to take a stroll around campus. A black Honda Accord drove past us. It was full of sorority girls. They were trying to get their faces in the air outside the windows. Their heads were like little minnows at the top of a minnow bucket. High-pitched giggles bubbled to the surface while ponytails like fins swished with the vibrancy and hope of lives yet to be lived. Then, unexpectedly, like countertransference, I was single, free, and lonely, all at the same time. I remembered how youth is wasted on longings, on dreams we'll never see. Thoreau noted mournfully, "The youth gets together his materials to build a bridge to the moon or perchance a palace or temple on the earth, and at length the middle-aged man concludes to build a wood-shed with them."

And in that moment, I realized I was the middle-aged man. It felt lonely. Because when all of the props of youthful dreams are taken away, we see our flabby faces in the mirror, and the red lines in the whites of our eyes that used to lead to an enchanted tale now lead back to only the view in the mirror. I saw in their eyes what I used to see in the mirror—the passionate expectation that something could happen in our lives. And isn't this where youth and middle age part company? One believes while the other becomes disillusioned. One is vibrant, the other is soured. On every inch of the sorority girls' guppy-like faces was expectant passion. On mine, weariness.

I guess this is what I divined as I stood across the street watching the girls in the Honda Accord. They didn't renew my belief that I could build a bridge to the moon. It wasn't that at all. It was the awareness that even though the moon is out of reach, God's travel plans were vibrant and alive with the feeling that he places us here for a reason.

I know God is in control of Blair's destiny. I told myself that as the Honda slowly but distinctively turned right at the end of the school's property and vanished.

THE LOST TOURIST WHO WORKED IN THE TOURIST OFFICE

After our tour of the campus, we decided to go see Square Books, which turned out to be a peach-looking storefront on the square with the latest John Grisham novel displayed in the window. We circled the square and passed a statue of a Confederate soldier on the lawn in front of the courthouse, a cattle truck sitting at a red light, and a sign that reads, "Tourist Office."

I said, "I want to go see William Faulkner's house."

Jill said, "You should go in the tourist office and ask somebody how to get there."

I was still skittish about the last directional debacle, so I finally talked her into asking. She was happy now that Blair was with us, so I got away with it.

Inside the tourist office on the square in Oxford, Mississippi, there was a faded newspaper clipping with Faulkner's picture. I pointed it out to Jill, who stood at a counter with Blair while a directionally challenged girl with pinkish-red lips looked for a map to Faulkner's house.

I motioned for Jill from where I stood reading the faded news clipping. She walked over and said, "What?"

"What is taking so long?"

"She's trying to find a map."

"A map to Faulkner's house? You mean she's clueless about how to get there?"

"Yep."

"You've got to be kidding."

"I found it!" the directionally challenged girl called with exuberance from behind the counter.

I couldn't believe it! It'd be like going to the Memphis tourist center to discover they don't know how to get to Graceland. We walked over to where she had the map spread out on the counter. She pointed to Rowan Oak, the name of Faulkner's house, and drew a line with her finger across University Avenue toward a street on the left.

Jill thanked her while I grabbed a free copy of the *Oxford American* that was being offered under the faded newspaper clipping.

When we reached the sidewalk, I told Jill that I couldn't believe what just happened. Somewhat ironic, since I couldn't find the university from University Avenue. I'm self-righteous. I'll admit it. I'm a hypocrite.

Post-it Note at the Edge of Faulkner's Yard

Faulkner's house sits at the back of a neighborhood that keeps it from escaping into the heart of Oxford. It was closed on Mondays. The place looked desolate. We parked anyway and made our way around a locked gate when suddenly a jogger emerged out of the woods, startling us. She never acknowledged our presence; she just ran past us.

We walked the length of the driveway. Overhead, an arching hedgerow of trees thinned against the sky. We stepped up on the front porch, cupped our hands to the entrance windows, and peered in.

Jill loves old houses. She said, "Take a look at this! It's *beautiful!*"

Blair sidled up next to me while I checked out what looked like an old horse trailer beside the house. The wheels were off, and the axles were resting on concrete blocks. I rounded the back of the trailer and discovered taillights that confirmed it was a horse trailer. I figured it belonged to Faulkner. Why else would someone put a horse trailer on blocks next to a historic site? While I was walking back to the front of the house, Blair reached out and hooked her arm inside mine, as if I was escorting her down the aisle of a church.

I knew the day was coming. I knew she'd soon not only leave the house for college, but she'd leave behind the tenderness of this moment at the edge of Faulkner's world to put her own face in the wind of destiny. Then she'll have her arm crooked around the arm of her husband, and old Dad will not be the main character anymore. I knew in the drama of her life, I'd be killed off. She'll get married, and those mornings when she sits at the kitchen table in front of me eating her cereal with a towel wrapped around her soggy hair while I write will come to an end.

She'll get married and end this moment when I'm the most important man in the drama of her life. Act II will begin, and I'll be the road less traveled. I know this. I guess that was why Jill and I wanted to linger at the edge of Faulkner's world a little longer. I guess that was why we stood in the brick maze of sidewalks under the massive magnolia tree in the front yard with Blair hanging on our arms a little longer. We wanted to hold on to this moment because we knew this trip to Oxford, Mississippi, would end.

As we listened to the wind in Faulkner's front yard, I realized that it was not Faulkner I was looking for at all, but God. I was hoping he'd emerge from the woods like that jogger and bring the assurance of his providence. He didn't. The one true and holy thing he offered was a Post-it Note: "Cherish the moment."

We didn't acknowledge it; we let silence speak. And when the world gets too cold and too large to comprehend, we can remember standing there. We'll remember how to get to Faulkner's house, even when the tourist office can't. We can remember that God spoke to us in the wind and in the moment about our transition, about how he controls destiny, even if it's revealed one moment at a time. Annie Dillard writes, "Experiencing the present purely is being emptied and hollow; you catch grace as a man fills his cup under a waterfall."[3]

We all walk where God's creation gestures quietly and savagely for us to stop and fill our cups. "For since the creation of the world God's invisible qualities—his eternal power and divine nature—have been clearly seen, being understood from what has been made" (Romans 1:20 NIV). So take the scenic route. Look for the hand that feeds the sparrow. Behold the beauty of the lilies, where "each moment is the fruit of forty thousand years ... and every moment is a window on all time."[4]

WATCH OUT FOR BUM PIGS!

How to Deal with Difficult People Along the Way

DEAN'S IN HIS FORTIES.[1]

He's a cowboy with a western shirt, Wrangler jeans, and a cowboy hat he removed before sitting down across the table from me. When I met him, he was coming off a bitter divorce. The ol' boy had been kicked to the curb a few times and was lonely and bitter. I was trying to be courteous, trying to be the good little pastor/family member, but he would have none of it. He wouldn't even acknowledge my presence as I sat in front of him at a family Thanksgiving dinner. The table was spread with bowls of food and aroma wafted between us. I smiled at him. But Dean was bent on excluding me, which was understandable.

I have over a hundred cousins, and there's just not enough time to build relationships the way you want to when you gather with a large family. About the time you learn Cousin Timmy's girlfriend's name, she's gone. You get to the point where you stop trying. I understand that. But what he said was inexcusable and mean spirited. When I asked Dean to pass me the sweet potatoes, he said, "I didn't come over here to serve you. I came over here to eat."

I have to say it took me by surprise. I didn't know what to say. He'd said it with cruelty dripping from his thick tongue. I knew he meant it, but didn't know why. If I'd maligned him in a sermon, it might've been justifiable. There was no such sermon. If I'd told his teenager to stop wearing Daisy Duke cutoff shorts to family get-togethers, then take me on. Get in my face. Take me out back and bare your knuckles. Do something that would hurt, but don't tell me, "I didn't come over here to serve you. I came over here to eat." It's juvenile, I know. You may have ignored him. You would've prayed for him.

After Dean's remark, an uneasy hush settled across the family table. We shooed it away. We have great shooing ability. Let a family squabble hit the shouting stage, and we'll get out our shooing devices and chase it into the next fight a week later, where it becomes a foundation for further shooing and a new act of denial.

Dean's closest relative, who had invited him, grabbed the bowl of sweet potatoes and hurriedly passed them to me. My brother, Kerry, smirked underneath a bowed head. He loved it and for days afterward gouged me with it and would even set up scenarios where he could repeat to me what Dean had said. He couldn't wait to get to family holiday meals so he could say it. I'd be enjoying family discussion at the table, not thinking, and I'd ask Kerry to pass something. A sly grin would stretch his face, and he'd say, "I didn't come over here to serve you. I came over here to eat."

I always laughed.

ALL IN THE FAMILY

All of us have someone inside the family or outside that we wish we could vote out of our lives. But the only way to deal with people who drive us nuts is to learn where and how they are pushing our buttons, because there are bum pigs in this world that we have to be on guard against. The apostle Paul had his, and we'll have ours. "Alexander the coppersmith has done me much harm, but the Lord will judge him for what he has done. Be careful of him, for he fought against everything we said" (2 Timothy 4:14–15).

Do you have any bum pigs in your life? Do you have any difficult people? There are those who enjoy doing you great harm. Bum pigs come in all different sizes and emotional makeups. Knowing how to relate, not only to God but to one another, is a key element of our spirituality. "Most important of all, continue to show deep love for each other, for love covers a multitude of sins" (1 Peter 4:8). It doesn't mean that you become a doormat for others to scrub their grimy feet across. But it does mean we have to get along the best way possible.

WHAT DO YOU CALL A CRAFTY PIG? A CUNNING HAM

Swine have been devastated at different times in history. Three little pigs built houses. Two were blown down. Then there's Porky Pig who has a problem saying, "That's all folks!" without stuttering. But pigs fare even worse in the Bible. They are husks for demons when Jesus casts them out of the demoniac, only to watch them do a swine dive into the sea. Then they become friends with the Prodigal Son, who's down on his luck and busted, so he takes a job feeding them, only to realize he's better off in his father's house, so the Prodigal Son returns home leaving the pigs behind. But pigs feel at home in the mud. They aim to get muddy and stay that way.

Most bum pigs have the following characteristics:

Prone to twisting the truth to benefit themselves.

Prone to rooting in other people's business.

Prone to trampling pearls.

Swine Behavior 1: Prone to trampling pearls.

A recent survey shows that the number one complaint people have at work is having to put up with critics.[2]

Critics steal our serenity by offering constant complaining and unwanted advice. Our response to a critic should be based upon what Jesus phrased as casting your pearls before swine. "Don't give pearls to swine! They will trample the pearls, then turn and attack you" (Matthew 7:6).

I walked into Dean's little game of trampling the pearls. He wanted me to be miserable like him. Swine behavior tries to rob your joy. Be careful not to combat others' hostility with anger that produces guilt and tramples sacredness. We have to learn self-control and the word "no" to accomplish this feat. It'll be one of the hardest things to do, but confrontation is not always a bad thing. And when you tell a swine person no, don't be surprised! She'll turn and attack you, trying to make you feel guilty, but you're in control of your own emotions.

The way to spot swine behavior is to look for the Porky Pig approach to solving problems. In the cartoon *Trap Happy Porky*, Porky Pig solves one problem by creating another problem. He has a mouse problem, so he gets a cat. Then he has a cat problem, so he obtains a dog. When we notice a person who's creating his own problems while dragging other people into them, we've discovered swine behavior.

The way to stay out of the path of swine that trample the sacred is by guarding our heart around certain people. Know what to reveal and what to conceal. Not everyone can be trusted with pearls. Some love the mud and like to sling it. We can't change that, but we can change our response.

The way to get free from the little hooves of turmoil is by following what Martin Seligman calls the ABCs. Seligman believes the healthy way to handle any critical stimulus is to stop and focus before reacting. He says:

It's a matter of ABC: When we encounter adversity, we react by thinking about it. Our thoughts rapidly congeal into beliefs. These beliefs may become so habitual we don't even realize we have them unless we stop and focus on them. And they don't just sit there idly; they have consequences. The beliefs are the direct causes of what we feel and what we do next. They can spell the difference between dejection and giving up, on the one hand, and well-being and constructive action on the other.[3]

A = *adversity*
B = *belief*
C = *consequence from this belief*

This is how it works:

Adversity: Dean says he didn't attend the Thanksgiving dinner to serve me.

Belief: I think, "This guy is trying to embarrass me."

Consequence: I feel hurt and rejected. I tell the family I'll never eat with him again.

Most of us live by the ABC method. We encounter an adversity, form a belief, and then suffer the consequences. The way Seligman says we should handle our adversities is to include another letter in this method. It's the letter D, which stands for Disputation—debating yourself on what is true in the adversity. The way to keep bum pigs from trampling our pearls is to plan for adversity by deciding to put all adversity through the ABCD method. Seligman believes that our first inclinations and assumptions are usually wrong. When you add the D step, it removes self from the equation, which keeps you from taking it personally.

With this added step, Thanksgiving dinner would have been much less traumatic for me:

Adversity: Dean says he didn't attend the Thanksgiving dinner to serve me.

Belief: I think, "This guy is trying to embarrass me."

Consequence: I feel hurt and rejected. I tell the family I'll never eat with him again.

Disputation or Debate: I tell myself that it's Thanksgiving and maybe Dean is feeling lonely and hurt. Divorce is not easy. He probably didn't mean it. Maybe his wife did all of the passing of food, and now that she's absent from his life, my asking brought back some bad memories. It wasn't personal. Dean doesn't hate me. He needs my sympathy.

I could carry the illustration further, but I think you see what I mean. Without the D in the ABC, sometimes we live without really questioning the validity of our beliefs. Seligman's ABCD[4] method can help us keep the critic at bay. We quench the emotional charge when we stop and focus on the adversity by disputing the validity of our beliefs.

Abraham gives us a portrait of how to deal with our supposed enemies. There's an incident in Genesis 21 in which Abraham makes a treaty with Abimelech, a pagan king. One of the interesting things about this passage is how Abimelech approaches Abraham: "About this time, Abimelech came with Phicol, his army commander, to visit Abraham. 'It is clear that God helps you in everything you do,' Abimelech said. 'Swear to me in God's name that you won't deceive me, my children, or my grandchildren. I have been loyal to you, so now swear that you will be loyal to me and to this country in which you are living'" (vv. 22–23).

Abimelech remembers what happened between the two of them in Genesis 20, and in his peacemaking he confronts Abraham's deception. Here's the background information about the deception in Genesis 20: Abraham was moving from place to place, fearful that pagan kings would kill him in order to take his wife, Sarah, into their harem. So wherever they traveled, Sarah and Abraham had a running lie that Sarah was to pretend she was Abraham's sister. Then their worst nightmare came true. When they traveled into Abimelech's kingdom, Abimelech checked Sarah out, liked what he saw, and inquired about her.

Abraham said, "Take her. She's my sister."

So Abimelech takes Sarah into the palace, and during the night, in a dream, God visited this pagan king and told him, "You are a dead man, for that woman you took is married" (Genesis 20:3).

Abimelech was both infuriated and relieved because he hadn't slept with her, and he called his royal officials to his side and revealed the situation and "great fear swept through the crowd" (v. 8). Why were they fearful? It seems strange. Maybe they feared Abraham because of Abraham's military history. In Genesis 14:1–16, Abraham armed 318 of his men and pursued and destroyed the combined armies of four eastern kings. And Abimelech may have been terrified because of Abraham's reputation. Who knows? But his opening line to Abraham in Genesis 21:22 was backed by history and bad blood.

James Montgomery Boice writes, "In all this there was plenty for which Abimelech could have despised Abraham. He could've said, 'Why, that hypocrite! He's always sounding off about God, but he's no better than we are. In fact, he's a good deal worse.' Yet this was not Abimelech's reaction."[5]

Abimelech could've blasted him or said some snide comment, like: "How's your sister, I mean wife, doing?" He could've put that little jab in and criticized him at the king's network luncheon. He could've spread rumors that would've been true. He could've said, "Have you heard what this prophet guy did to me last year?" Or he could've said, "The reason I don't go to church is because of this guy named Abraham who's supposed to be some holy man searching for the city whose builder and maker is God. Yeah, right! He's a liar, that's what he is."

When Abimelech said, "God helps you in everything you do," he disarmed the situation by offering a compliment. Abimelech put some thought into his approach. Maybe he took it through the ABCD approach of his day, thinking, *I need to make sure he knows I come in peace.* And sometimes all we have to do is bring peace. "A gentle answer turns away wrath, but harsh words stir up anger" (Proverbs 15:1).

On the other hand, there's a fine line between desiring to solve problems and wanting to be in control, so realize that some will never leave the mud or stop slinging it just because we respond to their criticism with a compliment. This is what hurts. So please guard the heart they are hurting. "Above all else, guard your heart, for it affects everything you do" (Proverbs 4:23).

Swine Behavior 2: Prone to rooting in other people's business.

Did you hear about the pig that fell in the mud? Don't tell anybody what I'm about to tell you, but—it got muddy. Seem juvenile? All gossip is schoolyard smack. When we hear juicy tales of gossip, we can't help but say, "Tell me more," because we feel we are being invited into an inner sanctum of secret tales. It's empowering and seductive. But it's an attempt to win friends by putting others down. Ernest Ligon writes, "An individual, then, who wishes to excel others, and tries to do so by gossip, uses the most hopeless type of compensation for his inferiority complex, because it implies that he has no hope of building himself up. He only hopes to bring others down to his level."[6]

When you encounter swine gossip, run, because you can be assured that when you are out of the swine's presence, he will gossip about you. This is swine MO. "They visit me as if they are my friends but all the while they gather gossip, and when they leave, they spread it everywhere" (Psalm 41:6). So think about how you'd feel if you knew this person was talking about you to someone else behind your back. This should rub us all the wrong way.

The way to deal with gossip is again to follow Seligman's ABCD method:

Adversity: Dean says he didn't attend the Thanksgiving dinner to serve me.

Belief: I think, "This guy is trying to embarrass me."

Consequence: After dinner, I begin to tell other family members how much I hate Dean and about how rude he was. Then I tell them what I've heard about him. "I heard his wife threw him out because he wouldn't find a job. He's lazy. Just look at him over there on the couch with that big belly lapping over his belt like he's nine months pregnant. I heard he didn't even graduate from high school."

Disputation or Debate: Pretend you're the family member I'm gossiping to at the family dinner. What are you going to do? This is where you have to debate whether to join in, defend Dean, or just grunt and act as if you didn't hear my tidbits of gossip, then change the subject. The latter approach is painful, but effective. It sends a subtle message that you're not interested, while not embarrassing me. And you better not embarrass me or I'll go blast you to someone else!

Creating lies is what swine do best. They sling mud, and I confess I felt like knocking Dean down a few notches. Maybe I'm doing that right now.

Swine Behavior 3: Prone to twisting the truth to benefit themselves.

Swine people have curly little tails that twist perception and truth in their direction. They turn our "wonderful expectation" into misery. And who wants to travel with a backseat control freak? The childlike question, "Are we there yet?" becomes a struggle over control, transforming the question into: "Are you going to travel my way?" All of us will face this type of swine behavior that tries to steal the joy from the journey.

One of the best stories on traveling with a control freak is found in Flannery O'Connor's *A Good Man Is Hard to Find*. A telling selection relates, "The grandmother didn't want to go to Florida. She wanted to visit some of her connections in east Tennessee and she was seizing at every chance to change Bailey's mind. Bailey was the son she lived with, her only boy."[7]

There always seems to be someone who isn't happy unless things are going his way. Les Parrott says, "Control freaks have these traits in common: obnoxious, tenacious, invasive, obsessive, perfectionist, critical, irritable, demanding, and rigid."[8]

Swine behavior can be very controlling. It's the tendency to twist things so that circumstances benefit them, and the grandmother in Flannery O'Connor's story was a control freak in the sense that she provided obnoxious unhappiness when everyone else was trying to be happy. Finally, John Wesley, the eight-year-old grandson said, "If you don't want to go to Florida, why dontcha stay at home?"

The grandmother's rebuttal was about an escaped convict named Misfit who was supposedly on his way to Florida. "Yes and what would you do if this fellow, The Misfit, caught you?"

Her ploy is fear.

John Wesley said, "I'd smack his face."

His sister June Star said, "She wouldn't stay home for a million bucks. Afraid she'd miss something. She has to go everywhere we go."

"All right, Miss," the grandmother said. "Just remember that the next time you want me to curl your hair."

Another ploy is taking love away, and it doesn't take the grandmother long to twist the vacation in her favor. She tells of an old plantation that she'd visited and recalls a secret panel.

"There was a secret panel in this house," she said craftily, not telling the truth but wishing that she were, "and the story went that all the family silver was hidden in it when Sherman came through but it was never found ..."

Of course the children wanted to see the house with the secret panel. John Wesley kicked the back of the front seat and June Star hung over her mother's shoulder and whined desperately into her ear.[9]

The grandmother's ploy here is the promise of something better than what is planned. Control freaks' ploys are fear, taking love away if their demands aren't met, and the promise of something better, which they can't always deliver.

The grandmother twists the vacation to fit her fancy with her tale of hidden treasure. She works underneath the situation to spark the children's imagination. Then she uses this underhanded, craftily told tale to sabotage the vacation. Control freaks will become victims if they don't get their way. It's swine behavior at its best.

Swine behavior can also work behind the scenes, extracting from you—one molecule at a time—the joy that was once your "wonderful expectation." They commence like a great artist, whose mind discerns the colors and the shadows of his fruit basket, sitting still, so still, so calm, then paints his vision of his subject. The shape emerges on the painter's canvas, and you know you're the fruit basket. Slowly, the life is drawn from you and rearranged into what the artist thinks is best for you. The artist believes you have to be protected from your distorted view of self.

Control freaks weave their lies so deep into our psyches that we can't differentiate between where we stop and the control freaks begin. We feel trapped on their canvas, stuck in the mode of their controlling tendencies, which makes us believe that without them we're nothing. We feel so guilty when they put us down or belittle the ones we bring into our lives. The stopping point, where is it? Sadly, it's only through confrontation with control freaks that we escape the canvas of what they want us to be.

Usually, we've allowed them control, and now it has to be taken back. But be wise. Control freaks will turn and trample and attack and twist the truth in such a way that you'll feel guilty for disagreeing with them. When we've allowed them to control us for years, then it will feel as if we have a huge void in our lives. We've depended on them to give direction, and now that we have to pick up the slack in that area, we feel overwhelmed. Stay with it. Turn your dependence and need of direction over to God, because moving away from the person who's controlling us can be done. In some cases, it must be done.

Sometimes we may need to move toward the one who holds us in bondage. We see this in the relationship between Abimelech and Abraham, which started out with a deception that never seems to leave Abimelech's mind. He's guarded when he approaches Abraham in Genesis 21:23: "Swear to me in God's name that you won't deceive me, my children, or my grandchildren. I have been loyal to you, so now swear that you will be loyal to me and to this country in which you are living."

Abimelech was smart enough to confront Abraham about his tendency to deceive. He laid it all out on the table with Abraham, letting him know that their relationship had to be built upon trust. He didn't go into a new treaty hoping that somehow the issues tied to the previous deception would magically work themselves out and go away. The hurt was still there, so he named it, and then set boundaries around the treaty.

The way to set boundaries around swine behavior is to be honest with the person about his tendency to control. Tell him where you draw the line. Set limits and don't back down. There's no easy way out. Confrontation is difficult and messy at times.

I look back on the incident with Dean and wish I'd had some comeback, something to shut him up and make myself look brilliant at the same time. I could've said a lot of things, but mostly I wish I'd said, "I wasn't talking to you."

THE WORLD WILL DROWN
YOU IF YOU LET IT

How to Stay on Top When You Hit Bottom

WE WERE ACCOSTED BY a deranged, tattooed, wrecker man on our first two-week vacation in the history of our twenty-year marriage.

It was July. Hot and humid. The road was moist with tar. Travelers exited the interstate while others joined our march to the sea. We were living the American adventure—bound for Panama City Beach, Florida.

Sloan was in the backseat watching a small television while Jill and I listened to Frank Sinatra. Sloan wanted to hang out with friends who were also vacationing in Panama City Beach. So when we arrived, we unloaded the SUV, then took Sloan to their condo. We parked in the center of the complex's parking lot—crowding in with seventy other cars—then took the elevator to the eighth floor of one of three high-rises.

We gathered with our friends on their balcony while I spouted some ridiculous clichés about how it doesn't get much better than this, about how a person can live his whole life without really seeing the true meaning of life. I said all of this while a humid coastal breeze flapped the towels hanging on the banister. Then we received a call from resort management requesting that we move our cars because a water main had burst in the parking lot.

I took my time getting up. *How urgent could it be?* I lazily made my way to the front balcony and gazed over to discover a geyser underneath *my* SUV. I panicked and flew down eight flights of stairs and hit the ground running. I waded through the gushing water, crawled in with water dripping from my feet, and cranked the engine. Then I put the vehicle in reverse and gassed it. When I did, the front end plunged! Six inches of pavement gave way, and the front of the SUV fell four feet into water and was going deeper while the faint commands of "Get out! Get out!" were being hysterically yelled at me.

I got out and watched my SUV drown in a sinkhole, the only victim in the parking lot. All the other cars made it out alive. I had to be the one who parked above the cracked pipe. That's the way things go for me, and I victimized myself while an audience of a hundred people gathered like midafternoon clouds. Their tanned faces were drawn tight for me. They hurt for me. They would not go away for me. They kept staring and staring and staring, and the more they stared the larger the crowd grew, until around seventy-five vacationers stood on curbs and in Bermuda grass in their baggy Tommy Hilfiger shorts and brightly colored swimsuits. And I felt naked. I knew it was just a car, but it was personal. It was as if the hotel maids—dressed in white and slumping over the balcony rails of the high-rise—were angels coming out of catacombs awaiting the death of my pride.

The public waterworks supervisor, a round little man, arrived first on the scene and started snapping Polaroid pictures of the sunken vessel, steering away from my "What are you going to do about this?" questions. I was thinking, *The insurance company is going to hook a wrecker truck to this soppy sucker, pull it out, and immediately start giving it floorboard-to-vacuum resuscitation. They'll keep it up until it spits all the water out. Then they'll park it in my driveway while it oozes funky, musty smells.*

MINE EYES HAVE SEEN THE GLORY
OF THE COMING OF THE WRECKER MAN

While I stood on the curb, I witnessed the glory of the coming of the wrecker man. He rolled in like a wild-eyed Southern aberration with tattoos covering both arms and stringy hair beneath a silver hat. When he spotted the crowd, he downshifted and let out on the clutch so the motor roared before coming to a stop. He jumped out and surveyed the crowd, looking intensely in all directions while his protégé exited the other side of the wrecker.

Then the police officers, the resort manager, the public waterworks supervisor, and the tattooed wrecker man put their heads together beside the sunken vessel to draw up rescue plans. When they broke from their huddle, the tattooed wrecker man yanked a chain from the back of his wrecker and hooked it to my new SUV. He checked for kinks, working his way back to the wrecker like a fisherman checking a trotline.

He crawled back in the '80 Chevy wrecker and fired the engine. It responded with smoke out the tailpipe. He put it in gear and gently eased out the clutch, pulling the chain taut. Then he floored the accelerator. The engine growled, *Vrooooom!* The tires spit out a wad of dust. The crowd sucked in their breath. Then ... the chain broke and the wrecker lunged across a curb while the chain whiplashed the side of the SUV!

The tattooed wrecker man was stunned. He cut the motor and desperately waded through water like a young cowboy after a calf being taken downstream. He fished for the chain in murky water and pulled it back to the bumper of my car.

I couldn't take anymore, so I approached him and shouted, "Stop it, mister! You're going to ruin my car!"

He got in my face and yelled back, "You take care of your business and I'll take care of mine! You got it?" It was courageous. A man bent on a mission to recover a vehicle no matter what the cost to the owner of the new SUV. And the police saved his hide, because they stepped in and said, "There will be none of this. Simmer down now!"

Don't Pull on Captain Wrecker Man's Cape

I backed away to let the tattooed wrecker man and his just-smoked-a-crack-pipe-on-the-way-over sidekick fix the chain and reattach it to the wrecker. (I'm cynical at this point and full of doubt.) He fired it up for another round, and this time he was unmerciful. He punished the wrecker for letting him down in front of the crowd that stood under a puffy-gray sky with nothing better to do than stare, and they stared and talked to each other out of the corners of their mouths. They did not want to miss the action. The chain creaked. The back tires pawed the pavement. The engine growled, *Vrooooom!* And ... the SUV responded! It emerged from the watery grave and slid across the lot to safety. And the crowd went wild! They cheered! They clapped! They loved him. He could do no wrong as he showered them with broad how-are-you smiles, and he leaned over to me in the hysteria of a sunken car being pulled to safety, and said, "I used to be a male dancer." Then he said in a *Grinch Who Stole Christmas* voice, "I know how to work a crowd."

I laughed. I have to admit it was hilarious. I have to admit that I liked him in that moment. I liked this guy who enjoyed his fifteen minutes of fame. He transformed before my eyes. The antisocial was welcomed back into society. What an eruption of joy! I was the village idiot, and he was Captain Wrecker Man! He was a superhero, and I was a superzero.

It's easy to become the victim who says to God, "Why did you do this to me?" It's easy to look around and view our relationship with God by comparing ourselves to others who are seemingly being blessed by God. Let someone we know hit a string of blessings and we'll blast him. And if we can't measure up, then we'll tear others down. We're a jealous bunch living in a jealous land, trying to keep up with the guy up the street with the golf tan and Jaguar with GR8LIFE on the license tag and who attends the Overcoming, Get Down, Boogie Slightly, Righteous Indignation, Altar-Calling, Conservative-Thinking Church of the Free Will.

So I accepted my fate and laughed. What else was there to do? Yank on Captain Wrecker Man's cape?

THE OPPOSITE

The choice of the tattooed wrecker man to wade back in for the chain that snapped, against the possibility that he might fail again, was something I didn't pick up on until the crowd cheered and he said, "I know how to work a crowd." I realized he was viewing the situation from the opposite end. He believed something good could be redeemed, even if he was trying to recapture the old feelings of being a male dancer. You have to hand it to the guy. He was rethinking the situation, doing the opposite of what I was doing, which was freaking out.

There's an episode of "Seinfeld" in which George Costanza is fed up with the way his life is turning out. He lives with his parents, has no job, and is in his thirties. So one day while sitting in a restaurant with Jerry and Elaine, he laments, "Why did it all turn out like this for me? ... Every decision I've made in my entire life has been wrong. My life is the complete opposite of everything I've wanted to be. Every instinct I have in every aspect, be it something to wear, something to eat, has been wrong."

Then, as if he's had a revelation, he stops the waitress who has taken his usual order and turned from the table and says, "I always have tuna on toast. Nothing has ever worked out for me with tuna on toast. I want the complete opposite of tuna on toast." The waitress walks off and George seems vindicated.

Then Elaine says a woman at the bar is looking at him. George responds, "So what. What am I supposed to do?"

"Go talk to her."

"Elaine, bald men with no jobs and no money who live with their parents don't approach strange women."

Jerry chimes in and says, "This is your chance to do the opposite. ... If every instinct you have is wrong, then the opposite would have to be right."

George takes the challenge to do the opposite and walks over to the woman at the bar. "Excuse me, I couldn't help noticing that you were looking in my direction," he says.

The woman says, "Oh! Yes, I was. You just ordered the same exact lunch as me."

George, in rapid-fire fashion, says, "My name is George. I'm unemployed and live with my parents."

A broad smile crosses the woman's face, and she says, "Oh! I'm Victoria. Hi."

It works! Doing the opposite got him a date with a beautiful girl, and as the episode builds, George reaps good fortune for doing the opposite.[1]

If pleasing the crowd has been our life to this point, then doing the opposite is the right thing to do. Trying to live by God's moral choices is doing the opposite of our sinful instincts. It's what C. S. Lewis calls building up the "real central man," the part of us that will live in eternity. Lewis writes:

> People often think of Christian morality as a kind of bargain in which God says, "If you keep a lot of rules I'll reward you, and if you don't I'll do the other thing." I do not think that is the best way of looking at it. I would much rather say that every time you make a choice you are turning the central part of you, the part of you that chooses, into something a little different from what it was before. And taking your life as a whole, with all your innumerable choices, all your life long you are

slowly turning this central thing either into a heavenly creature
or into a hellish creature.[2]

Life is a struggle between two value systems, God's and the
world's, and we must choose. "Don't copy the behavior and customs
of this world, but let God transform you into a new person by changing the way you think" (Romans 12:2). Changing the way we think
means that we have to rethink, and rethinking who we are can be a cat-
alyst for change, but we're afraid of what we'll find in the dark crevices
of our agony. "Some people say they want to change their lives, but all
they do is sit around waiting for some *outside* event or person to come
along and rescue them."[3]

The only way transformation takes place is by beginning to make
choices. When we interpret life as a choice between morality and
deception and choose morality, we are submitting our soul to the
scrutiny of the light that may not be fully understood until eternity. So
when we begin to make moral choices, such as choosing to tell the
truth when it'd be easier to lie, then the "real central man" is built up.

CHASING THE WORLD BY ITS TAIL

Every problem we face will produce an emotion. The key to overcoming our problems is to rethink the emotion we feel. Is it a true emotion?
Is my response the right one? This will force you to look at the problem
in the opposite way. Roger von Oech writes, "Imagine that you're a
parking meter. How does it feel when coins are inserted in you? What
is it like when you're 'expired'? How could you be easier to use?"[4]

Thinking of yourself as a metaphor, as some object that places your
thoughts outside of you, is a way to do the opposite. "And yet, LORD,
you are our Father. We are the clay, and you are the potter" (Isaiah
64:8). The metaphors of the clay and the potter are great examples of
looking at our relationship with God based on metaphors.

When we choose a metaphor from which to view life, it is usually grounded in a value system—the world's or God's. Trying to win the approval of the world is the dark choice away from the "real central man." Paul says, "Obviously, I'm not trying to be a people pleaser! No, I am trying to please God. If I were still trying to please people, I would not be Christ's servant" (Galatians 1:10). Paul wasn't advocating rugged individualism. He was letting the Galatians know that his apostleship came from God and not people. Matthew Henry writes, "But Paul was a man of another spirit; he was not so solicitous to please them, nor to mitigate their rage against him, as to alter the doctrine of Christ either to gain their favor or to avoid their fury."

Paul knew how to work a crowd. He'd built a reputation for it. He'd held the coats of those who'd stoned Stephen to death. As Saul, his identity was wrapped up in his public persona of persecuting Christians. And Ernest Ligon believes self-esteem is tied to the way an "individual sees himself and how he thinks others see him, [which] are powerful determiners of his behavior."[5]

For Paul to give up the power to wield persecution was a deep psychological response that we seem to gloss over. When a person wraps his identity around behavior, he's seeking a way to derive his self-worth. Because when measuring up becomes identity, then the childhood question "Are we there yet?" becomes "How can I derive my worth from the crowd?" Answering this question is like chasing the world's tail. We'll never catch it or win its approval.

Erik Erikson, a psychologist concerned with identity, believes we learn to "win recognition by *producing things*."[6]

Self-worth and identity are associated with our jobs, our status, our wealth, the kind of car we drive, the gated community we live in—those things the world applauds. It's a life judged by the way we believe others perceive our achievements and/or failures. And a crowd's response can produce either self-worth or self-doubt.

The tattooed wrecker man knew "working the crowd" meant he

had to accomplish something to get them to applaud. His mere presence on the condo's property garnered no respect. It filled no hole. But when he succeeded, they responded. But why did he have such an overwhelming urge to perform? Karen Horney says of someone like the tattooed wrecker man, "This is his unconscious tendency to rate himself by what others think of him. His self-esteem rises and falls with their approval or disapproval, their affection or lack of it."[7]

It probably started on some stage in the recesses of late-night adult entertainment. Maybe in the beginning he felt adored, felt that the world was noticing him for the first time. But in the end, maybe things got treacherous. Maybe when he put his clothes back on at the end of the night, he felt the loneliness of the sunrise that exposed him for what he truly was—a man seeking attention, attention that may have been withheld in childhood. There may be a hole there. Who knows? It makes one wonder why he left an occupation that he still bragged about to handle the world's fender-benders and stalled cars. But give him credit. He recognized the potential of the moment. He seized it and got his fix of the world's applause. And if his behavior was strange, then the crowd's response was just as bizarre. They went nuts! You would've thought he had saved the *Titanic* and hundreds of lives!

We live in a world that doesn't have a lot to cheer about, because to applaud a tattooed wrecker man—who'd turned my misfortune into a reason to "work a crowd"—was to cheer for something the crowd realized a vacation in this world would never offer, which is redemption. Redemption took place in the parking lot. We can't deny that. It was on a different level, but so was the response.

BREAKING FREE FROM THE WORLD
C. S. Lewis believed that the physical part of the human body will fall away at death, leaving the "real central man," causing us to "see everyone as he really was. There will be surprises."[8]

I like that last line. I think that's what surprised me about the tattooed wrecker man. He was antisocial on the surface, but deep down he sought approval and an entrance into a social world that up to that moment had excluded him. Sure, he had a husk of weathered and tinted skin. He was no Cub Scout. But emotionally and psychologically, he was working for his own medals and awards, trying to please a world that would step away from the curb of a misfortune, only to forget him. But not me.

If I had about ten thousand tattooed wrecker men, I'd change the world. Because if you can find people with the desire for applause and introduce them to the Holy Spirit, turning them into "real central men," they'll become passionate for the applause of the only One who counts. And whenever you receive applause from the audience of One, you'll never go back to pleasing men. Just ask Paul. He knew an audience of One produces the one and final statement about our tenure here on earth—"Well done, my good and faithful servant." So we wait for the day when Christ will rescue us from where the world has collapsed and from where we have fallen, never to drown again in the pain of sorrow.

MILKING THE MOMENT

Most wrecker men would've pulled the SUV out with no fanfare, taken the check, and called it a job, but not my tattooed wrecker man. After he hooked the SUV to his wrecker for the long haul back to the shop, he did a victory lap. I promise you, he did. He drove around the condominium complex with his arm waving out the window, as if he were in a parade, and the sad thing is the crowd cheered him again. He milked the moment for all it was worth. And he's probably still milking it in some auto-body shop in Panama City Beach: "Yeah, when that guy yelled for me to leave his car alone, I got in his face and told him I'd yank a knot in him." (He does a Barney Fife sniff and straightens his silver hat.) "Yeah, that old boy shuffled back to the curb. He didn't want any of me. Then I yanked that sucker out just as smooth as you please. And the crowd went wild! I had them eating out of the palm of my hand. Right here," he says, stabbing an open palm with a stubby finger.

SUFFERING ALONG THE WAY

Why God Allows Pain

THE OUTPATIENT WAITING ROOM was near capacity at Crestwood Medical Center in Huntsville, Alabama. Our chairs faced each other. Our feet shuffled around on the beige carpet as we waited for our names to be called. I was waiting to have a CT scan to see if the leg pain I'd been having was a tumor somewhere in the pelvic area pushing against a nerve.

We had faces of concern. Some nodded off with chins resting on their chests. Others were holding magazines or books, flipping pages and peering over the tops every now and then. Donny and Marie Osmond were interviewing Bob Barker on the television mounted on the wall, which was turned up just enough to let you catch this word ... that word ... this word.

Facing me, a woman served a cup of coffee to her husband and then took a seat beside him. They were in their sixties, senior citizens who were getting familiar with the insides of hospitals. We were trying not to stare at one another, trying not to diagnose each other's reason for being there. Mostly, we looked at each other's feet. The man had red socks that clashed with the rest of his clothing.

I glanced at the television. Bob Barker was playing "Let's Make a

Deal" with Donny and Marie. The show's applause and laughter wafted through the room like the musty truth that the world was still finding things humorous and praiseworthy in the face of our sickness.

A young nurse who looked like an actress on "General Hospital" approached carrying three large cups as if she'd been to the concession stand and was returning with something to quench my thirst. The doctor ordered them, but these cups were not thirst quenchers. These cups contained an evil potion, and she shoved them at me with unsympathetic eyes.

"You've got an hour and a half to down all three cups."

"You're kidding."

"You should be able to drink one every thirty minutes."

"Okay," I said peering over the tops of the cups to see a swirling brew, a substance that looked like plaster of paris for an art class project.

"I'll return in an hour and a half."

That was it. She turned and walked off, leaving me with three cups of faux plaster of paris to choke down, while the man in red socks stared at me.

GOT MILK?

I raised the first cup to my lips, tilted it into my mouth, swallowed, almost choked, rebounded, gulped, and then set it back with its companions.

The man in red socks snapped out of his catatonic trance and pointed to my three cups of homemade chalk wine, as if his condition wasn't as severe as mine, and said, "That's going to be quite a feat to drink all three of those."

I smiled and sipped and watched the clock and sipped some more, watched the clock and sipped. I was thinking, *God, please let me get these three cups down before my hour and a half is up.*

An hour later with two down and one to go, the man in red socks said, "Well, son, you 'bout got it whupped now."

I smiled at my new friend and got up to go to the bathroom. His feet danced a slight nervous jig. He didn't ask where I was going. We weren't that close, but I asked him if he'd watch my cup. "Don't let anybody drink my last cup while I'm gone," I joked.

He chuckled and said, "Son, I don't think anybody wants to drink your cup."

And in a way, that old man was right about a lot of things in life. Nobody wants to drink the cup of suffering, especially if it belongs to someone else. But in the hands of the doctor, the homemade chalk wine became a tool to make my flesh glow, uncovering the truth about what was taking place inside, about where the pain originated.

Within the human soul, the tool God uses to uncover our true character is suffering. God exploits evil in much the same way doctors exploit radioactivity. Something bad becomes something good. "And we know that God causes everything to work together for the good of those who love God and are called according to his purpose for them" (Romans 8:28). But who wants to suffer?

CATFISH ARE JUMPING

While attending school at Gordon-Conwell Theological Seminary in South Hamilton, Massachusetts, I would sometimes go with my family to sightsee in Gloucester. Gorton Foods is located in Gloucester, and the smell of fish wafts through this quaint coastal town. It was during this time that I learned how important codfish are to business as we watched fishing boats chugging in to port under the weight of their famous and delicious catch.

There's a large market for eastern cod, especially in regions farthest removed from the northeast coastline, but the public demand posed a problem to the shippers. At first they froze the cod, then shipped them elsewhere, but the freeze took away much of the flavor. So they experimented with shipping them alive, in tanks of seawater, but that proved even worse. Not only was it more expensive, the cod still lost its flavor and became soft and mushy. The texture was seriously affected.

Finally, some creative soul solved the problem in a most innovative manner. The codfish were placed in tanks of water along with their natural enemy—the catfish. From the time the cod left the East Coast until they arrived at their westernmost destination, those ornery catfish chased the cod all over the tank! When the cod arrived at the market, they were as fresh as when they were first caught. There was no loss of flavor, nor was the texture affected. If anything, it was better than before.[1]

Got any catfish in your tank? Are you feeling defeated and hopeless? Sometimes things that seem hopeless are in our tanks to keep our souls from getting soft, mushy, and tasteless, and it's the way catfish are used that makes this method of shipping seem evil to codfish.

The way God uses the problem of pain in the world, extracting something good, is the mystery of suffering. I believe evil exists, but the determining of what's evil and what's God's goodness can be tricky. C. S. Lewis writes, "To ask that God's love should be content with us as we are is to ask that God should cease to be God: because He is what He is, His love must, in the nature of things, be impeded and repelled by certain stains in our present character, and because He already loves us He must labour to make us loveable."[2] And in light of God's discipline to make us loveable, we have to realize that "our real enemy is not our suffering itself."[3] What might seem as suffering to us may, in fact, be God making us loveable.

When the Urge Strikes

How God's goodness can be mistaken for suffering came to life for me a few years ago when my daughters started asking for a puppy. Blair, my elder daughter, would get the Sunday paper and open it up to the classified section, and with all the dramatics she could muster in her voice, she'd read the listings for pets.

"Boxer puppies: 2 white and fawn males, 3 brindle females," she'd say with color-commentator cadence.

My family wanted a dog, but I didn't think we needed a beast. So I talked them into buying a Jack Russell terrier, and we brought this intellectual giant with a midget body into our home when it was six weeks old and lovingly named it after my favorite preacher, Spurgeon. Then the challenge to house-train this puppy began. I followed Spurgeon and pounced on Spurgeon. If there was even the appearance of evil, I yelled at the innocent puppy with a cowering ability to melt your heart with fear. But training is training and the process continued, even when it seemed evil to Spurgeon.

My attempt to train the puppy to go outside was in conflict with its natural instinct that any place is just as good as another when the urge hits, whether in the living room or the hall. Its instincts were opposite of what I was training it to do. The puppy was pure puppy that had to be transformed into a domesticated house pet, and the process was discouraging at times because a good three months into the training, around Christmas, Jill received a nice comforter for our bed as a gift from my mother. Jill spread it out and called me into the room to admire her gift, and someone else crept into the room undetected.

When we exited the room, the trespasser found the comfort of the comforter and the urge hit. It wasn't a pretty sight—not the stained comforter, but the look on Jill's face, and I didn't think Spurgeon would live to see another doggy treat. But Spurgeon had an advocate with Jill—a beloved friend named Sloan, my younger daughter. Sloan knew that Spurgeon had been appointed once to die and the doggy-angel of death was at Spurgeon's food bowl, so Sloan interceded on Spurgeon's behalf, saving the puppy, causing Jill to have mercy, thwarting plans to tie Spurgeon to the bumper of the Isuzu Rodeo for a long trip through the countryside.

My work was cut out for me if Spurgeon was going to remain a resident at the Stofel house. I scolded the puppy, trying to teach it not to have the urge on things that belonged to Jill. To keep the puppy smelling fresh and pleasant, I bathed him, which had to be confusing to the cowering, shivering animal, and as C. S. Lewis wrote, "It would seem to cast grave doubts on the 'goodness' of man,"[4] because when the scolding starts or the sudsy washing begins, the puppy doesn't understand that these things make him into a loveable creature. But with the training over, Spurgeon is admittedly a whole lot better off than if he lived in the wild. Because as I write, Spurgeon, the once unlovable puppy, is a well-trained sleeping machine sacked out on a $75.00 L.L. Bean bag and no longer fears being dragged behind the Isuzu Rodeo. All is well with the contents of the house. No more urges in the wrong places.

Suffering can be misunderstood. God's goodness may seem harsh because we don't understand that "what we would here and now call our 'happiness' is not the end God chiefly has in view: but when we are such as He can love without hindrance, we shall in fact be happy."[5]

THE PARABLE OF THE MILKY CREEK CAN RACE

The Bible doesn't answer every question about suffering or about why hospitals litter the world. It simply says, "So if you are suffering according to God's will, keep on doing what is right, and trust yourself to the God who made you, for he will never fail you" (1 Peter 4:19). The "suffering according to God's will" is the part we don't understand. Why a good God makes us or allows us to suffer is baffling, and the divine discipline mentioned in Hebrews 12:7 (NIV), "Endure hardship as discipline," is the biblical concept of training, instruction, and firm guidance.[6]

I liken it to a can race in the milky creek that ran through the middle of Green Acres subdivision, where I grew up in Franklin, Tennessee.

The creek flows from a nearby rock crusher and is milky and undernourished. Nothing much lives in it, except maybe a crawdad or two, but the creek was the center of life for us kids. It was where we learned how to maneuver our bicycles around the path that runs parallel to the creek. Every game we played took place around the creek. It was part of us. For kids need a place to be kids, and we let the creek define who we were. We wore it on our clothes. We tasted it on our lips, washed our bikes in its substance, and held can races in the milky runoff. We'd find a can and a long stick, then we'd stand at the water's edge, and on the count of three, toss our cans. We'd take our sticks and guide those cans around debris, pushing them past undercurrents, knocking them away from the bank, trying to keep them on course to the finish line.

In the parable of the milky creek, we are the cans, and the water represents free will. God's will is depicted by the stick, which is his loving arm of correction that he uses to make us into the likeness of his Son. "My child, don't ignore it when the Lord disciplines you, and don't be discouraged when he corrects you. For the Lord disciplines those he loves, and he punishes those he accepts as his children" (Hebrews 12:5–6). God's discipline can feel like God's wrath, but it's really His loving arm of correction that he uses to work his redemptive process in our lives. It's a lifelong process that must be entered into by humbling ourselves under his loving arm of correction, and when we do, the goodness of God works in us the culmination of our salvation.[7]

He prods us away from the banks of the past, points us in the direction of faith, and pushes us past sinful pitfalls, steering us around fallen human nature. Although he never uses his stick to beat us, he sometimes has to strike the water to get us moving again, to get us unstuck, but he never strikes out in anger at those trying to find his perfect will. God always gets us moving as gently and lovingly as he can, and the method he uses depends on our cooperation and humbleness.

God longs to make something good out of our bleak, frightening experiences by working beneath the layer of suffering to extract his grace, turning trials into divine moments when he approaches and causes all things to work together for good.

Sometimes bad things happen to good people. These bad things are not personally our fault. Death, in and of itself, is not directly our fault. Hurricanes are not our fault. These evils caused by the Fall are not how God makes us Christlike, which brings up another aspect of the milky creek can race because, due to the terrain of the creek, sometimes our cans would drop down a waterfall, fill up with water, and sink. Sometimes evil happens. Having a can sink was part of the race because the creek wasn't perfect. We raced in a fallen creek. This is a crude illustration, but I believe it depicts how a fallen world takes victims for no apparent reason. God leaves the terrain intact unless he wants to work a miracle—God is God and can do what he wants—but rarely does he change the terrain of the world and its laws, such as gravity.

The world has been affected by erosion and entropy due to the Fall, just as humans have been affected by sin. God works out his purpose with his loving arm of correction and doesn't eliminate the free will of the water. He compensates by making something good come from evil. Sometimes bad things happen, just as when our cans filled up and sank in the waterfall. We never purposely filled our cans with water; we tried to spare them, tried to keep them safe as best we could. And just as we wanted our can to win, God wants us to keep moving. "Let us run with perseverance the race marked out for us" (Hebrews 12:1 NIV).

OVERANALYZE THIS!

After my hour and a half was up, the "General Hospital" nurse came to get me. I was smiling, exposing white teeth and a chalky tongue. I'd defeated the three cups of evil potion. I'd placed them in a dark chamber where only a CT scan could find them, and the medical technicians arranged me on a bed that moved through a tunnel. The swirling, humming machine sucked me into its bosom, and a voice from heaven said,

"Hold your breath." So I held my breath until I felt I might explode, then the voice from heaven said, "Breathe."

This exercise of "Hold your breath—breathe" went on for a while, until the woman who brought the three cups of potion pulled the IV out of my arm and asked, "The only thing you've had to drink or eat is what I've given you, right?"

"That's it."

"Okay. You're free to go," she said sweetly. She walked me to the door, and I started thinking about what she asked me: "Is this the only thing you've had to drink or eat?"

Oh, no, she's seen some big mass. Maybe at first she thought I'd been eating, but now that she knows I haven't been eating, she knows it's a tumor. This is it!

When I got home from my CT scan, I collapsed on the couch.

"What's wrong with you?" Jill asked.

"I might be dying," I said.

"Dying?"

"Yep, dying."

"From what? What did the doctors say?" Her face tightened.

"The technician performed the CT scan, and then she asked me if I had had anything to eat or drink besides what she'd given me. I think she must have spotted something and wanted to make sure it wasn't a jelly roll or something."

"Robbie, you are overanalyzing. She probably wanted to make sure you followed procedures."

Okay, maybe I was overanalyzing my cup of suffering, and when we overanalyze, the world around us stops. The joy of seeing a sunset ceases. The sun rises and sets, and we never notice. When we overanalyze, the world stops. Joy is killed.

To rekindle the initial excitement of the childhood question is to know God can exploit evil. He can transform suffering into something that contours our soul for eternity. Spurgeon says, "Evil is transformed to good when it drives us to prayer."[8]

So please don't get stuck on the bank of having to know the answer to *why*. It can't be answered fully. It only creates in us the Job complex. For Job wanted an explanation for his affliction, but God did not offer clarification. In the moment of Job's suffering, he only received the miracle of God's face. "My ears had heard of you but now my eyes have seen you" (Job 42:5 NIV).

DRINK UP!

There's an element of suffering that goes along with a fallen world. Then there's the misunderstanding of God's training. May we have the discernment to know the difference. I believe this was Christ's prayer when he prayed, "My Father! If this cup cannot be taken away until I drink it, your will be done" (Matthew 26:42 NIV).

Sometimes the way we go forward is by drinking the cup of suffering. The rest belongs to God's will.

BOAT LAUNCHING CAN BE
HAZARDOUS TO YOUR EGO

When Your Dream Boat Won't Float

MY FATHER WAS TRAVELING down a back road in rural Williamson County, Tennessee, when he spotted it sitting in somebody's front yard for sale. As soon as he laid eyes on the little wooden fixer-upper, he knew he could make her float with some elbow grease and new boards in the bow. So he slammed on the brakes of his '70 Chevy truck, threw it in reverse, and backed to the edge of the road. He sat there with his elbow stuck out the window, sucking his teeth, just looking at it—enthralled with a vision of being behind the wheel on Percy Priest Lake while my mother stretched out on the bow, sunbathing in her bikini. Maybe he saw himself as Captain Ahab chasing down a few Moby-Dick rockfish.

He offered the man fifty dollars less than what he was asking, and the man about snatched his arm off trying to get the money. We went home that day with the little wooden boat trailing along behind us like a new puppy.

It had a metal steering wheel beneath a glass windshield and a flag attached to a pole in the back, which could have been a pirate's flag or an American flag, I can't remember. But to an eleven-year-old boy, that little wooden boat glittered with the riches of His Majesty's ship on the high seas. But my father had a hard time getting it out of the driveway once he parked it.

Of course, my mother said, "Billy, you have no business trying to fix that piece of junk. You don't know what you're doing. You've never owned a boat."

My father didn't listen. He was a man with a project. While the boat sat in the driveway on its trailer, he sanded, painted, repaired, and caressed it. Every afternoon he could be found transforming the neglected boat into a raft that would float down his own Mississippi to freedom.

I'd climb aboard and pretend I was motoring over the water, the sun at my back, and good-looking women surrounding me. I'd turn the steering wheel toward the stars and then back toward some planet beyond the Milky Way. Sometimes I'd pretend to be marooned on that island with Mary Ann and Ginger while my father, the Skipper, fixed the hole in the SS Minnow so we could go home.

THE LAUNCH

The launch date arrived on a Saturday. My father took off early from work and hooked the trailer with the little wooden boat to the back of his truck. Then he had to talk my mother into joining us. She did, but only after he promised he wouldn't "knock all of the water out of the lake."

"I promise. We'll find a quiet slough and stay put ... but if the fish ain't bitin', we got to move to another one."

"No, you'll find ONE and sit there. No running me ragged. I just got my hair fixed. You'll have me looking like Lucille Ball." My mother felt her hair as if she were taking its temperature.

"All right, let's go, but I ain't leaving at no three in the afternoon just because you think that's when the sun goes down."

My mother ignored this statement, and the rules of engagement were set. She wasn't thrilled about owning a boat, but she was willing to go along if it meant she could get a suntan. So we headed out for Percy Priest Lake in Nashville. We dipped and swerved with the road as my father cut corners and let the play in the wheel slip through his palms. The two of them sat in different worlds while the interstate hummed beneath the recapped tires.

The ramp my father had in mind for his maiden voyage was two miles past the dam. When we arrived, it was cluttered with fishermen geared up like soldiers in their high-powered bass boats. They appeared to be going to some holy war beyond the buoys. None of it fazed my father. The bigger the crowd, the more he'd have as an audience.

"Get out and guide me down," he said.

He opened the door and I slid out across the bench seat. I crossed in front of the truck. The smell of the radiator. The sound of belts turning. I positioned myself at the back of the boat and started waving him back. He eased the little wooden boat down the ramp as if it were a forty-foot yacht.

"Easy. Easy. A little to the left. Keep her straight. Come on back," I said, as the ruts in the concrete bumped under the tires and water oozed up the sides of the little wooden boat. Then I yelled, "Stop! That's good."

My father climbed out of the truck and unhooked the chain with a glow on his face. My mother and I climbed aboard while he tied us off at the bank and left to park the truck. We sat in the boat and waited and watched the traffic looping in and out of the boat dock—a big Ford, a one-ton pickup with a barking dog standing on a toolbox in the back, motorcycles, and old men in their pickups with nothing better to lose than time.

The sun was at my back. I had my shorts on, shirt off. No good-looking women beside me. Still, it was great. Then we noticed water under our feet. We looked beneath them as if it were all a dream. Then our feet were submerged. The little wooden boat was taking on water. *Mayday! Mayday!*

By the time my father reached the boat, we were going the way of the *Titanic*. The bow was up, the motor was bubbling water into its crankcase, and Mother was screaming, "Billy, get us out of here! Billy, you do something! Billy! I told you you didn't know what you were doing!"

With the help of some concerned men, he pulled the little wooden boat out of the water. Saved us. Saved the boat. He was, however, unable to save face. My father's dreamboat was a sinker. Yet he was a champ that day, for as people watched with panic on their faces, he was calm and patient. His persona communicated that things were under control, but underneath he was embarrassed standing there on the shore with a boat that wouldn't float, a boat you could not trust to do the very thing it was made to do.

My mother berated him during the sixty miles back home. She pushed him close to the edge of retaliation, but he stayed the course. He never saw this coming. He never intended to sink his wooden boat, but the unintended consequence seemed worse than the actual sinking because my mother vowed to never set foot in his boat that was "taking up space in the driveway." And my father suffered the consequences of the unintended. He never set out to break my mother's trust in his boat repair expertise, but the damage was done. The unintended outweighed the intended.

It's hard to know when this will happen. No one can plan for all the variables in life—just ask Jephthah. He never intended for his daughter to be the first to walk out of his house when he bargained with God. "He said, 'If you give me victory over the Ammonites, I will give to the LORD the first thing coming out of my house to greet me when I return in triumph.' ... When Jephthah returned to Mizpah, his daughter—his only child—ran out to meet him, playing on a tambourine and dancing for joy" (Judges 11:30–31, 34). It was an unintended tragedy. Who knows what he thought would meet him first when he got home? His dog? His mother-in-law? There are just too many variables to make such a rash vow. But it's safe to say that certain situations have unresolved conflict that comes out as unintended consequences. My mother and father weren't really fighting over the boat debacle. Unresolved conflict fueled the spat. It became the unintended consequence—another reason to continue the fighting that eventually led to divorce.

BEWARE THE UNINTENDED

An Olympic coach of a leading crew team prepared his crew by inviting a meditation instructor to teach awareness techniques. He hoped the training would enhance their rowing effectiveness. As the crew learned more about meditation, they became more synchronized, there was less resistance, and their strokes became smoother. The irony is that they went slower. It turned out that the crew became more interested in being in harmony than in winning.[1]

Understanding the unresolved conflict uncovers the true problem, whether it's unresolved conflict in a marriage, a workplace, among our children, or in our churches. Karen Horney poses this question about dealing with unresolved conflict: "What do unresolved conflicts do to our energies, our integrity, and our happiness?"[2]

According to Horney, they diffuse our energy, waste our time, and deter our happiness, because the unconscious is constantly trying to solve these conflicts, which inevitably slows us down and exhausts us, requiring lots of sleep. We see this in Elijah's life after he runs from Jezebel: "Then he went on alone into the desert, traveling all day. He sat down under a solitary broom tree and prayed that he might die. 'I have had enough, LORD,' he said. 'Take my life, for I am no better than my ancestors.' Then he lay down and slept under the broom tree. But as he was sleeping, an angel touched him and told him, 'Get up and eat!' He looked around and saw some bread baked on hot stones and a jar of water! So he ate and drank and lay down again" (1 Kings 19:4–6).

Elijah was exhausted and afraid. Yes, he'd outrun a chariot for seventeen miles. Yes, a great victory will deplete your body. But his problem resulted from unresolved conflict that came from a message Jezebel sent Elijah after God slaughtered the prophets of Baal: "So Jezebel sent this message to Elijah: 'May the gods also kill me if by this time tomorrow I have failed to take your life like those whom you killed'" (1 Kings 19:2). It was a threat he couldn't resolve. Maybe Elijah had his eyes on himself. It's strange that he'd feel like this after such a great victory at Mount Carmel. But he did. He chose to live with unresolved conflict instead of facing the threat. He needed to settle in his spirit the sense of divine protection.

Clovis Chappell writes, "Jezebel's threat totally upset the prophet's sense of victory. He came to feel that he had not won after all. For the first time he gave way to fear. Cowardice rushed upon him and drove him, without rest, down the road that led into the wilderness."[3]

Unresolved conflict leads to the wilderness. It causes us to "disqualify the positive," which is "drawing conclusions only from that part of the evidence that is negative."[4] Elijah is a prime candidate. He told God, "I have zealously served the LORD God Almighty. But the people of Israel have broken their covenant with you, torn down your altars, and killed every one of your prophets. I alone am left, and now they are trying to kill me, too" (1 Kings 19:10). There's nothing positive in this speech. He disqualified it. "Yeah, there was a victory at Mount Carmel, but. ..." He dropped back to the unresolved conflict concerning Jezebel. It was the old trail through emotional terrain. Elijah needed to "beware the unintended."

Unresolved conflict can immobilize us. The way to break free is to first name the unresolved conflict. We do this by eliminating the possibilities of why we're in conflict. We have to pinpoint the cause.

My parents could have realized that they were probably struggling over control in the marriage, allowing it to bleed over into the boat incident. Unresolved conlflict will color our future intentions. So eliminate surface strife by getting to the root of the problem. *Why am I frustrated? Am I really upset over another issue?* Horney believes that this type of questioning will help us do "the opposite of lying or of putting the blame on others."[5]

ANNALS OF MARINE HISTORY

My father talked my mother into giving him one more shot at taking a cruise on the boat that wouldn't float. Maybe they'd resolved some conflict since the last trip. I know he'd gone on and on about how it was his fault. He missed one board in the bow. "It was no big deal, Pat. So you got your feet wet. Come on ... one more trip. I'll sell it if it doesn't float."

My father got another shot at his moment in the annals of marine history. We all loaded up and headed for the lake. Again he backed the little wooden boat down the ramp. Again he eased her down like a forty-foot yacht.

"Easy. Easy. A little to the left. Keep her straight. Come on back," I said, standing at the back, as water oozed up the sides of the little wooden boat.

He jumped out of the truck and unhooked the chain with a glow on his face. He hoped she would float. My mother and I climbed aboard. We hoped, too.

The sun was at my back, my shorts on, my shirt off. Then it happened. *Bubble, bubble, bubble.* Our feet were submerged again beneath the thick green water. It just bubbled right back in—twice in a row. The boat that wouldn't float still wouldn't float. My father's dreamboat was still a sinker. His hopes were dashed on the rocks of despair, but he didn't give up.

He saved his money and waited until another dummy bought that little wooden boat from our front yard. Then he put a big down payment on a fiberglass boat—one of those brown fishing boats with black speckles mixed into the paint. It had a picture of a big jumping bass on the side, and man, would it float. It floated on a cushion of air so thick that my father looked like a low-flying eagle. If you were watching my father from the shore, you'd have thought he was a spaceship, just hovering over the top of the water—a magic carpet ride.

My father got to the bottom of his boat problem. When he got to the end of his boat expertise, he discovered he still had options. Most people stop pursuing their dreams because they feel the road is blocked. They see no option except hopelessness. But the way to resolve any problem is to look for viable options. The way to open up to these is to admit that you've traveled the wrong road. As Maeterlinck says, "In owning our faults we disown them; and in confessing our sins, they cease to be ours." Confession makes us what Paul called "a new creation" (2 Corinthians 5:17).

For my father it meant admitting that he couldn't fix the boat. So he weighed his options and decided to save up for a new boat. He did something positive. He didn't allow failure to immobilize him.

FOUR LEPERS WHO KEPT HOPE ALIVE

Four lepers in the Old Testament found themselves in a hopeless situation. They were going to die a miserable death, so one spoke up and said, "Why should we sit here waiting to die?" It was a great question—one for the ages, not just for lepers. Everyone has to answer this question, because all of us are on a deathwatch. Time is short. Yet we sit and fritter away our present moments while waiting for something bigger. It's always something bigger for us. It's never enough. You hit the lottery; you live! So we think. You sit here on your behind; you die. Not much different, is it? Both are an excuse to escape the present.

The four lepers planned on turning themselves in to the enemy, thinking maybe they would be fed. But when they arrived in the enemy's camp, the army was missing. The army had fled when the Lord made it sound like "the clatter of speeding chariots and the galloping of horses and the sounds of a great army approaching" (2 Kings 7:6).

They discovered an empty camp, and "they went into one tent after another, eating, drinking wine, and carrying out silver and gold and clothing and hiding it" (v. 8). The lepers failed to factor God into their hopelessness.

They were looking for relief and found God at work. When Christ is at the center of our lives, Philippians 4:6 takes place in our hearts. Let this verse be your prayer. " Don't worry about anything; instead, pray about everything. Tell God what you need, and thank him for all he has done."

Hang in there, because one of these days you're going to have a life that floats in areas where it has been shot through with holes. If you wait upon God, he will do more than fix the holes. He will bring you the hope of a new life. So don't "become weary in doing good, for at the proper time [you] will reap a harvest if [you] do not give up" (Galatians 6:9 NIV). One day, your life will soar on wings like eagles. For "even youths grow tired and weary, and young men stumble and fall; but those who hope in the Lord will renew their strength. They will soar on wings like eagles; they will run and not grow weary, they will walk and not be faint" (Isa. 40:30–31 NIV).

My father hoped one day to have a boat that would float, and he did. He did the hard work of saving and waiting. He never quit dreaming, never failed to hope, and never stopped waiting. He overcame his adversity, and I'm sure, somewhere, written in the sky, was a Post-it Note from God: *Billy Stofel kept hope alive.*

WHEN YOU CAN SEE ONLY
WHAT YOUR HEADLIGHTS REVEAL

Shine Your Faith into the Darkness

I HAVE VOICES IN my head. Tiny voices. These voices try to convince me that I'm in the dark, that I have no clue what's going on. When I leave church at the end of the day, I'll lock the door and get in my truck, and the voices in my head tell me I didn't really lock the door. "Go back and check the door. You didn't lock it," the voices say to me. "Someone is going to break in and steal things." So I check. I'm responsible. I go back and grab the knob and try to turn it—of course, it's locked.

Sometimes the voices show up while I'm in the pulpit. The voices say, "Booorrring."

And somewhere between the introduction and point one, someone will validate the voices by checking his watch or yawning. "See. Somebody just checked his watch. This is bad!" the voices say. Then they make snoring sounds.

We've all heard these voices that deliver thoughts of hopelessness. Everyone has moments when thoughts of defeat enter and the future goes black. We lose our vision and can see only the circumstances in our headlights, but this is when we should shine our faith in the darkness and refuse to live by emotional reasoning, which is a type of worrying that says, "I feel it, so it must be true."

Hanamel, the prophet Jeremiah's cousin, was a man who faced ominous circumstances and was unable to step into the darkness beyond his limited sight. He focused on the circumstances surrounding the Babylonian siege of Jerusalem and let the actions of the king of Babylon rob him of his faith.

Oceanfront Property in Jerusalem

In Jeremiah 32, we find the army of the king of Babylon sweeping down on Jerusalem, and Hanamel was sitting on a piece of property that was about to be scorched. Maybe he'd been tipped off. Who knows? But one thing for certain, he knew disaster was imminent, so he called on his cousin, Jeremiah, and begged him to buy the field that was getting ready to be ransacked by the Babylonians, because all Hanamel could see was what was in his headlights—looming doom. So Hanamel seeks out his cousin, Jeremiah, and an absurd transaction occurs: "Then, just as the LORD said he would, Hanamel came and visited me in the prison. He said, 'Buy my field at Anathoth in the land of Benjamin. By law you have the right to buy it before it is offered to anyone else, so buy it for yourself'" (Jeremiah 32:8).

I don't think Hanamel was working off the fair disclosure clause. It'd be a lot like Scarlett O'Hara selling Tara—house and all—when she sees the Yankees marching through Georgia. It would be like Scarlett O'Hara saying to herself, *Scarlett, the Yankees are coming, and you've got to sell Tara before they burn it to the ground.*

Hanamel was concealing the fact that the field was worthless, the field was getting ready to go the way of Atlanta and its environs during the Civil War, and maybe the voices started in his head: "You're going to lose all you have. The Babylonians are going to burn your barn and scorch your field. Go look out the window. Here they come!"

Maybe Hanamel obeyed the voices and ran to the window and

pushed back the curtains to find ... nothing unusual. A bird sailed above his barn and a purple sunset eased into the edge of his vineyard, while the wind rustled a fig tree. He sighed, let go of the curtain, and moved slowly across the room to get a cool drink out of a cistern. He mumbled to himself about all the work he'd put into the field. *All that plowing for nothing. Putting up with that stubborn ox. Now this!* He took a drink. Then the voices started again.

"You're a loser, Hanamel. You've never been able to do anything right. Just look at you. You're a tired old man with nothing to show for it, and your field is getting ready to be scorched by the Babylonians. All that work—gone."

"All right, all right, enough already! ... Perhaps I can sell my farm before the invading army gets here."

"Oh, yeah! That's a good one! Who's gonna buy this doomed piece of ash?" the voices scolded.

"Jeremiah will buy it!"

And he did, but if you look only at the absurd purchase, then you'll miss the faith of Jeremiah, you'll miss how he shone his faith into the darkness, because he had the faith to say, "For the LORD Almighty, the God of Israel, says: Someday people will again own property here in this land and will buy and sell houses and vineyards and fields" (Jeremiah 32:15).

How many of us would have plopped our money down in hopes that one day the land would be returned to our possession? How many of us would have bet our souls against history? Jeremiah stood there in the doubt of the moment before the invading army swept through to ransack and blister, thinking, *One day this field will prosper.*

Anyone can say, "Sure, it's possible. The field could fall back into Jeremiah's possession." That's mere talk. No action. But could we put our money down? All of us are hanging on tightfisted to our dollars. Not Jeremiah. Even though it was an economic downturn in a time of war, he still believed in redemption.

I found myself at one point of my life worrying about the bills. I'd just graduated from Middle Tennessee State University with a degree in psychology, and I'd been working at the inner-city mission for three months, teaching Bible studies and providing general pastoral counseling. For three years, I watched men come and go. Some found the help they were seeking, while others found the soup bowl and a spoon. It can leave you jaded when you pour your life into people, only to see them choose failure over and over again.

I was trying to get my mind around the whole concept of how to work with crack addicts, and Sister Brenda, the woman who ran the program, was mentoring me daily. I was a rookie counselor with a big heart and a huge student loan, and the job was not paying the bills, but for some inexplicable reason, the inner-city mission was where God wanted me.

It was tough. My wife and I struggled to find purpose and redemption in a job that placed us just above the poverty line. We had frequent conversations about how we might have missed God, especially when the bills were due. It became a source of contention between us. We'd lie awake at night and discuss our alternatives. God calls us to live wisely, but there are times when we have to take a step outside the beam of our headlights.

F. W. Boreham wrote: "No man needs to be sure of everything. ... The captain of a ship, bringing his vessel into port through a haze or a drizzle, does not need to see all the trees and the houses along the shore; ... if he can distinctly make out one or two fixed landmarks he can proceed with confidence."[1]

Jill and I proceeded with confidence and distinctly made out one or two fixed landmarks, the greatest being when I met Joseph, a crack addict who came into the mission with a dejected posture and defeated eyes. Nothing about him demanded the redemptive act, but God set us both up.

THE CRACK WHERE THE LIGHT SEEPS IN

The morning I met Joseph, I'd decided to resign. I needed to move on to something that paid better, that offered a little more security. So that morning I headed to work, rehearsing in my mind what I'd say to Sister Brenda. I steered the Accord toward the exit where the Tennessee Titans play in their new stadium and worried about the circumstance I'd leave her in. I wasn't the greatest counselor, but I'd been willing up to this point. I was learning, so I knew Sister Brenda would be disappointed.

I wiggled free from the car and walked beneath a basketball hoop that loomed over cracked pavement. The net was swaying in the cold December wind as I pushed my way through the metal door into the sanctuary.

"Hey, guys. How are you doing this morning?"

Some spoke, others just smiled as I walked past them on my way to Sister Brenda's office. Once inside her office, I slid my skinny frame into a chair in front of her desk. I was ready to give my resignation.

"Good morning."

"Are you okay?" she said, reading my wooden face and strained movements.

"Yeah, I'm fine."

A knock at the door interrupted the conversation.

"Sister Brenda, could I see you for a minute?" said Joseph, an African-American man in his late forties.

"Joseph, I want you to meet someone who will be involved in your progress."

Sister Brenda turned to look at me while I struggled to my feet. I stuck my hand out and a calloused hand limply grasped mine. His eyes were seismographs that measured the earth in front of him.

"Nice to meet you, Joseph." I sat back down in the chair.

He didn't say anything. He stood there—sinew hanging on tired bones.

"Joseph, I'll talk to you when Robbie's Bible study is over."

He turned and walked out with his eyes focused on his shoes, and I thought to myself, *If this man changes, then I'll know there's a God.*

"I'm hoping Joseph will stick with the program," Sister Brenda said.

"Yeah, me too," I said, standing. "Well, I guess I'll round everybody up for the class." I was slated to give a group Bible study in ten minutes and decided that my resignation speech could wait until after the Bible study. There was no need hatching a conversation that would need more than ten minutes.

I began the Bible study by telling them if they'd seek first the kingdom of God, then the things they needed would be added unto them. I was trying to make myself believe it.

I said, "See these shoes I have on?" I held one foot high in the air and shook it as if I were doing the Hokey-Pokey. I put my foot down. "They were given to me by a man who sells shoes for a living." It sounded clever, and they craned their necks to get a better view. I continued, "I have a friend who wins shoes by meeting certain quotas, and guess what—he wears the same size shoe as I do. He wins shoes and I receive the blessing by the boxload. If you follow God, he will take care of you in ways you'd never imagine."

While I was saying all of this, I heard the voice of hopelessness say, "Yeah, right. Sure he will."

I scanned their faces to see if they believed, thinking about my conversation with Jill the night before, about telling her I would resign. "I'll a find a job with real pay," I'd said.

I continued and the words got stuck in my throat. I cleared it and said, "I have so many shoes, I brought a pair to give away." I dangled a pair of green-and-white Reebok tennis shoes by the strings. I asked, "Does anybody here wear size 8?"

Joseph, the new, little, dejected man was smiling now. He looked up for the first time and raised his hand.

I walked back to where he sat and said, "Here are your shoes."

We continued with the Bible study and toward the end, Joseph raised his hand to speak.

I said, "Yeah, what is it, Joseph?"

He said, "Last night that preacher talked to us about prayer." He stopped and looked around the room as if he were looking for someone to finish for him.

"What preacher?" I said.

Tommy, one of the guys sitting in the circle, said, "You know, the little retired minister who comes in on Monday nights to give us a Bible study."

"Yeah," said Joseph, "He said that if we needed anything that we should pray and ask God for it. So last night I prayed for a pair of shoes."

No one moved. We were stunned. We had to change the way we viewed him. We knew something had taken place beyond us. It took a minute to get our souls back underneath us, because when a man—who knew no God and lived only to draw crack into his lungs—received an answer to a prayer we would not even think about praying, it frightened us the way it frightened the people of Gadara to see the demoniac dressed and in his right mind. Joseph laced up the Reeboks that day while we all took turns touching them, hoping whatever was in his prayer that was now on his feet would somehow bless our own lives.

Those shoes became a symbol of God's providence in the life of a crack addict, and Joseph graduated from the program later that year drug-free. He got a job at a nearby factory and rented an apartment. His life changed because he knew if God could hear him about a pair of shoes, then he could hear him concerning the rest of his life.

I went home and told Jill about the green-and-white Reeboks. She listened intently as I told her about the way he prayed and God heard, and a few days later she met me at the mission for lunch to get her own look at the shoes.

"Jill, this is Joseph, the man I was telling you about who prayed for a pair of shoes. Hold your foot up here, Joseph. Let Jill see the answered prayer."

Jill reached out and rubbed the back of her fingers across the lace and said, "You're a blessed man, Joseph."

He smiled and hung his head, like a little boy in the first grade being praised by a teacher. Then I got out my camera and snapped a picture of him wearing those shoes.

God's mercy toward Joseph translated into a new outlook, a renewed sense of courage and poise. Joseph, like Jeremiah, shone his faith into the darkness and found God faithful and discovered the redemptive act.

Act III

It's the hope we have on a vacation, the hope that we'll finally arrive, hope that we'll get to see the beach and the crashing of foamy waves. My brother and I would always rise up from our Old Maid game or whatever it was we were doing besides guarding our designated space that Mom had marked off with her finger around the hundred-mile mark.

"If the two of you don't stop fighting ..."

"He's leaning on me, Mom."

"Kerry, get off of him. Now both of you settle down. I'm going to mark off your space, and you'd best not cross it."

So Mom would mark the bench seat in the back and we'd cower into our space. We were always afraid that one was going to get away with something, so when he crossed my line, I squealed on him.

"Mom, he crossed the line."

Mom would reach around and try to whip him with light smacks of her hand, which made us laugh and made her madder. But when we saw the ocean, it didn't matter anymore. Kerry could lean over in my space and get a look from my window and vice versa. The belittling and the fighting and the blaming of body odors and the cheating at Old Maid were all gone when we beheld the ocean. We remembered why we had come. Sometimes we, too, need to remember why we are on this journey. We're on this journey to get to the place where nothing seems to bother us when we behold the beauty of the destination, and even though it's not in view, God gives us glimpses. He opens the window for a brief moment to let us know that eternity does exist.

I guess that's what we all sensed the day I took the shoes to work with me. It was a glimpse of redemption. For "the grace of Christ is constantly working miracles to turn useless suffering into something fruitful after all."[2]

If this is true, then we should silence the thoughts that tell us otherwise. When we dwell only on the mistakes we've made, it allows Satan's lie to be planted in our hearts—"You cannot change. It's hopeless." And if we allow ourselves to feed on this negative voice, we'll remain hopeless and helpless.

I heard Haddon Robinson give the following illustration in a sermon at Beeson Divinity School:

> People who write drama have a formula. The formula says that:
>
> Act I—You get your hero up a tree.
> Act II—You put a bear under the tree.
> Act III—You kill the bear and get the hero down from the tree.

> Whatever can be said for that simplistic formula, one thing is certain. You never judge a play by its second act. You dare not assume that in the second act the bear has won. You and I, who are followers of Jesus Christ, are men and women who live in the light of God's final act.[3]

Hanamel based his land deal on Act II. Jeremiah based his purchase on the redemption found in Act III of the Babylonian drama.

We need to realize that even though we stand waist deep in a field of thorny problems in a land of captivity, that in the light of redemption, in the light of Act III, the vineyard will one day blossom; it will blossom into subdivisions and schools and the activity of the redeemed.

The exiles returned from Babylon and reclaimed their farms, and George Buttrick writes, "Jeremiah's real estate deed was not lost, for the Scriptures record it, and you and I discuss it with a whimsical smile, saying to each other: 'He bet his soul against history.' If only the deed were in some museum this morning, and we could go to see it! I think if we could see it, then we would take a new grip on hope, on courage. The whole episode is a [shadow] of the Cross of Christ."[4]

Buttrick states that what happened in Galilee and on a cross and at the Resurrection will one day become a field where souls flourish and the downtrodden receive their redemption. "It shall come back in finer form—every last good."[5]

Anybody care to buy some oceanfront property in the afterlife? Anybody want the deed to it? "I have one to offer: the Christian faith."[6]

It might not look like much now, but one day it will become a kingdom where souls find their rest. Anyone want to lay down his life for this deed?

WHERE DO YOU WORK?

I worked at the mission with those crack addicts for the next three years, and when Jill and I thought we might go under financially, we'd remember the shoes. I'd tell her the story about how Joseph raised his hand and about the way he laced them up, while those other broken souls stared at raw redemption. When I finished telling Jill, we'd stare at the ceiling above our bed and enjoy the thoughts of how God answered the prayer of a man who'd done nothing before that moment to earn it, other than he shone his simple faith into the darkness. He was a failure by the world's standards, but God unveiled a divine plan of redemption that was as simple as a pair of Reeboks and so intricate that certain details, unguided, would have thwarted the mission.

On nights when money was low, we'd think about Joseph, then we'd turn to each other in bed, and Jill'd say, "Where do you work?"

I'd say, "I work at an inner-city mission."

She'd grab my hand and say, "You're a blessed man, Robbie Stofel."

I'd say, "You're a blessed woman, Jill Whitehurst Stofel."

Then we'd turn the light out and sleep like babies.

APPENDIX

Life is a journey littered with detours, roadblocks, limited sight distance, places to wait, and other obstacles that hinder our progress toward becoming Christ-like. As adults, we replace the childlike question—"Are we there yet?"—with questions of worry and doubt: "God, why aren't we there yet? How much longer will I have to wait for the fulfillment of my dreams?" Sometimes we allow the circumstances of our lives to become points of contention with God. As you look back over the principles applied in this book, think about how your present circumstances can be transformed. First, look upon your trials as being temporary in the big picture of eternity. It will help you differentiate between what is important for eternity and what's not, which will produce a "wonderful expectation" for the final destination. Second, by using this study guide you'll be able to reflect on each road sign at critical points on the journey. This will help you concentrate on areas of your life that need to be submitted to the process found in Romans 5:3–5: "We can rejoice, too, when we run into problems and trials, for we know that they are good for us—they help us learn to endure. And endurance develops strength of character in us, and character strengthens our confident expectation of salvation. And this expectation will not disappoint us." Enjoy the journey through this study guide.

NOTES

Chapter 1: Stop Signs, Red Lights, and Other Places to Wait

1 QuickVerse 7.0 Standard, Matthew Henry's Commentary on the Whole Bible (Omaha, Nebr.: FindEx.com, 2000), note on Exodus 13:18.

2 Jamie Buckingham, *A Way Through the Wilderness* (Grand Rapids, Mich.: Chosen Books, 1983), 55.

3 Sue Monk Kidd, *When the Heart Waits* (San Francisco: HarperSanFrancisco, 1990; HarperCollins, 1992), ix.

4 Matthew Henry, *Matthew Henry's Commentary on the Whole Bible*, ed. Leslie F. Church (Grand Rapids, Mich.: Zondervan Publishing House, 1961), 676.

Chapter 2: Construction: A Way of Life

1 Rosamund Stone Zander and Benjamin Zander, *The Art of Possibility* (New York: Harvard Business Press, 2000; New York: Penguin Books, 2002), 104.

2 Ernest M. Ligon, *The Psychology of Christian Personality* (New York: Macmillan, 1953), 295.

3 Arthur Freeman and Rose DeWolf, *Woulda, Coulda, Shoulda: Overcoming Regrets, Mistakes, and Missed Opportunities* (New York: William Morrow, 1989; New York: HarperPerennial, 1990), 58.

4 David Foster Wallace, "Good Old Neon," in *The O. Henry Prize Stories 2002*, ed. Larry Dark (New York: Anchor Books, 2002), 371.

5 Ralph P. Martin, *Word Biblical Commentary*, vol. 40, ed. David Hubbard (Dallas: Word Publishers, 1986), 318.

6 Charles Reynolds Brown, *Finding Ourselves* (New York: Harper & Brothers, 1935), 11.

Chapter 3: Yielding to Life's Demands

1 Warren W. Wiersbe, *Be Hopeful* (Wheaton, Ill.: SP Publications, 1982), 11.

2 Eric Berne, *Games People Play: The Psychology of Human Relationships* (New York: Grove Press, 1964), 101.

3 Karen Horney, *Our Inner Conflicts: A Constructive Theory of Neurosis* (New York: W.W. Norton & Company, 1945; reprinted, 1992), 155.

4 Zander and Zander, *The Art of Possibility*, 104.

5 Martin E.P. Seligman, *Learned Optimism* (New York: Pocket Books, 1992; New York: A.A. Knopf, 1991), 15–16.

6 Ibid., 44.

7 D. Martyn Lloyd-Jones, *Spiritual Depression: Its Causes and Cures* (Grand Rapids, Mich.: Eerdmans Publishing Company, 1965), 21.

8 Charles Haddon Spurgeon, *Spurgeon's Expository Encyclopedia*, vol. 8 (Grand Rapids, Mich.: Baker Book House, 1978), 299.

9 Gordon D. Fee, *The First Epistle to the Corinthians* (Grand Rapids, Mich.: Eerdmans Publishing Company, 1987; reprinted, 1991), 461.

10 Frederick Buechner, *Going on Faith: Writing as a Spiritual Quest*, ed. William Zinsser (New York: Marlowe & Company, 1999), 52.

11 Jack Kerouac, *On the Road* (New York: Penguin, 1999), 47.

Chapter 4: Going Your Own Way

1 Aaron Beck, *Prisoners of Hate* (New York: HarperCollins, 1999), 27.

2 Joseph Epstein, *Snobbery: The American Version* (New York: Houghton Mifflin, 2002), 16, 20.

3 Ibid., 23.

4 Beck, *Prisoners of Hate*, 31.
5 Zander and Zander, *The Art of Possibility*, 104.
6 Epstein, *Snobbery*, 279.
7 Os Guinness, *God in the Dark* (Wheaton, Ill.: Crossway Books, 1996), 62.

Chapter 5: We'll Leave the Light on for You
1 Harry Emerson Fosdick, *On Being a Real Person* (New York: Harper & Brothers, 1943), 143.
2 C. S. Lewis, *Mere Christianity* (New York: Touchstone Books, 1996), 88.
3 Harry Emerson Fosdick, *Riverside Sermons*, quoting Wordsworth (New York: Harper & Brothers, 1943), 143.

Chapter 6: Highways Will Get You Only So Far
1 Dietrich Bonhoeffer, *Life Together* (New York: Harper & Brothers, 1954), 19.
2 Ibid., 36.
3. Charles Haddon Spurgeon, *The Treasury of David*, ed. Roy Clarke (Nashville: Thomas Nelson, 1997), 1,366.
4. J. Harry Cotton, *Hebrews—Exposition Chapter 10*, vol. 11, ed. George Arthur Buttrick (Nashville: Abingdon Press, 1955), 713.
5 Bonhoeffer, *Life Together* (New York: Harper & Brothers, 1954), 18.

Chapter 7: Detours, Shortcuts, and Roadblocks
1 Freeman and DeWolf, *Woulda, Coulda, Shoulda*, 39.
2 Ibid., 40.
3 Fosdick, *Riverside Sermons*, 55.

Chapter 8: When You Feel Life Slip-Sliding Away
1 Freeman and DeWolf, *Woulda, Coulda, Shoulda*, 45.
2 Ligon, *The Psychology of Christian Personality*, 233.

3 Ibid., 222.

4 D. T. Howard, "A Functional Theory of the Emotions" in *The Wittenberg Symposium on Feelings and Emotions* (Worcester, Mass.: Clark University Press, 1928), 143, quoted in Ligon, The Psychology of Christian Personality, 222.

5 Ibid., 222.

6 Charles Swindoll, *David* (Dallas: Word Publishing, 1997), 43.

7 Brown, *Finding Ourselves*, 5.

Chapter 9: Is Life Beautiful? I Can't Ever Tell

1 Frederick Buechner, *The Hungering Dark* (New York: HarperCollins, 1969; New York: Harper & Row, 1985), 73.

2 T. Dewitt Talmage, "The Botany of the Bible; or, God Among the Flowers," in *500 Selected Sermons*, vols. 1–2 (Grand Rapids, Mich.: Baker Book House, 1900; reprinted, 1956), 89–100.

3 Annie Dillard, *Pilgrim at Tinker Creek* (New York: HarperCollins, 1998), 82.

4 Thomas Wolfe, *Look Homeward, Angel* (New York: Charles Scribner's Sons, 1929; reprint, 1995), 3.

Chapter 10: Watch Out for Bum Pigs!

1 If you call me, I'll tell who he is. But I have an unlisted number. Plus, I may be bitter, so we'll just call him Dean.

2 Les Parrot III, *High-Maintenance Relationships: How to Handle Impossible People* (Wheaton, Ill.: Tyndale House Publishers, 1996), 2.

3 Seligman, *Learned Optimism*, 211.

4 Seligman takes the model further by adding an "E," which is "Energization." Energization is the energy we feel as we succeed in dealing with negative beliefs.

5 James Montgomery Boice, *Genesis*, vol. 2 (Grand Rapids, Mich.: Zondervan, 1985; Grand Rapids, Mich.: Baker Book House, 2002), 669.

6 Ligon, *The Psychology of Christian Personality*, 304.

7 Flannery O'Connor, *A Good Man Is Hard to Find and Other Stories* (New York: Harcourt Brace Jovanovich, Publishers, 1948; reprinted, 1983), 9–10.

8 Parrot, High-Maintenance Relationships, 77–78.

9 O'Connor, *A Good Man Is Hard to Find*, 17.

Chapter 11: The World Will Drown You if You Let It

1 "The Opposite," "Seinfeld" episode 86, broadcast May 19, 1994, VHS video.

2 Lewis, *Mere Christianity*, 87.

3 Freeman and DeWolf, *Woulda, Coulda, Shoulda*, 85.

4 Roger von Oech, *Creative Whack Pack* (Stamford, Conn.: U.S. Games Systems, 1992), card 29.

5 Ernest Ligon, *Dimensions of Character* (New York: Macmillan Company, 1956), 13.

6 Erik Erikson, *Identity and the Life Cycle* (New York: International Universities Press, 1959; W.W. Norton & Company, 1980), 91.

7 Horney, *Our Inner Conflicts*, 54.

8 Lewis, *Mere Christianity*, 87.

Chapter 12: Suffering Along the Way

1 Charles Swindoll, *Illustrations Unlimited*, ed. James S. Hewett (Wheaton, Ill.: Tyndale House Publishers, 1988), 14.

2 C. S. Lewis, *The Problem of Pain* (New York: Macmillan, 1962; New York: Simon & Schuster, 1996), 33.

3 Charles Swindoll, *Hope Again: When Life Hurts and Dreams Fade* (Dallas: Word Publishing, 1996), 252.

4 Lewis, *The Problem of Pain*, 39.

5 Ibid., 43.

6 William L. Lane, *Word Biblical Commentary*, vol. 47B, ed. John D.W. Watts (Dallas: Word Publishers, 1991), 420.

7 "He will keep you strong to the end, so that you will be blameless on the day of our Lord Jesus Christ" (1 Corinthians 1:8 NIV).

8 Charles Haddon Spurgeon, *The Treasury of David*, updated by Roy H. Clarke (Nashville: Thomas Nelson, 1997), 766.

Chapter 13: Boat Launching Can Be Hazardous to Your Ego

1 von Oech, *Creative Whack Pack*, card 42.

2 Horney, *Our Inner Conflicts*, 154.

3 Clovis Chappell, *Sermons on Biblical Characters* (New York: Richard R. Smith, Inc., 1930), 119.

4 Freeman and DeWolf, *Woulda, Coulda, Shoulda*, 54.

5 Horney, *Our Inner Conflicts*, 171.

Chapter 14: When You Can See Only What Your Headlights Reveal

1 F. W. Boreham, *The Last Milestone* (London: Epworth Press, 1961), 45.

2 Thomas Merton, *No Man Is an Island* (New York: Harcourt Brace & Company, 1955, renewed 1983), 92.

3 Haddon Robinson, *Good Guys, Bad Guys, Us Guys*, audiocassette, Eighth Annual William E. Conger Jr. Lectures on Biblical Preaching (Birmingham, Ala.: Beeson Divinity School, 2000).

4 George Buttrick, *Sermons Preached in a University Church* (New York: Abingdon Press, 1959), 33.

5 Ibid., 36.

6 Ibid., 36.

READERS' GUIDE

For Personal Reflection
or Group Discussion

READERS' GUIDE

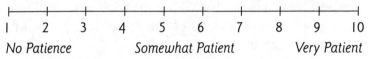

Chapter 1:

"Stop Signs, Red Lights, and Other Places to Wait"

1. Robert writes, "This childlike question has been driven from us and replaced with a question of doubt, 'God, why aren't we there yet?'" What is one situation where you've felt like asking God this type of question?

2. Waiting is difficult. No one likes to wait. What are some of the things you do to help alleviate the stress of waiting? Mark an X on the scale below indicating how patient you see yourself.

```
|———+———+———+———+———+———+———+———+———|
 1    2    3    4    5    6    7    8    9   10
No Patience        Somewhat Patient      Very Patient
```

Read: Exodus 13:17

3. God led the Children of Israel on the long route instead of through Philistine territory. Discuss why this was important for the success

of the Exodus. Will God put us on the long route to save us from ourselves?

4. Maybe you are longing for something to happen in an area of your life. Do you think God has it "in the garage," waiting for the appointed time when he will present it to you?

Read: Psalm 90

5. Moses probably penned this psalm as a prayer to be used daily by the people in their tents or by the priests in the tabernacle-service in the wilderness. Describe how you might use Psalm 90 to keep from feeling overwhelmed.

Group Prayer Suggestion

Take time to pray for your group members who feel overwhelmed and need patience. Pray this Scripture for them: "... give us hope and encouragement as we wait patiently for God's promises" (Romans 15:4).

Chapter 2:
"Construction—a Way of Life"

1. We all hide our weakness, our darkness, our ugliness, and our fallenness from other people. Why do you think we do this? Have you ever hidden some aspect of who you are because you felt embarrassed about it?

2. Sometimes we worry more about our image on the journey—the style of car, having the right clothes, the big house—more than we do the condition of our souls. What are some of the possible consequences of being an "image manager" who worries about appearance?

Read: 2 Corinthians 10:12

3. Paul refuses to compare himself with others. He believes it's a foolish thing to do. Discuss why Paul believes this is foolish. When have you compared yourself to someone else? How did you feel?

4. David Foster Wallace's protagonist discusses what he calls the "fraudulence paradox," which hypothesizes that "the more time and effort you put into trying to appear impressive or attractive to other people, the less impressive or attractive you felt inside—you were a fraud." In what ways is this true in your life?

Read: 1 Samuel 16:7

5. Discuss why God looks upon the heart and not appearances.

Group Prayer Suggestion

Take time to pray for your group members who are feeling like they don't measure up to others or even to their own *idealized self*. Comfort them with the fact that God looks upon the heart.

Chapter 3:
"YIELDING TO LIFE'S DEMANDS"

1. Robert writes, "Everyone yields to something." Are you learning to yield to things that are out of your control?

2. The first ingredient in the recipe Robert designs this chapter around is the act of scattering your problems before you to see which ones carry eternal significance. How can you implement this principle to reorganize the priorities of your life?

3. The second ingredient in the recipe of overcoming our problems

is the act of smothering the urge to limit life to this world only, meaning we should be in the world but not of it. How do you separate the two realities of living in the world, but not of it?

4. Martin Seligman, in his book, *Learned Optimism*, states, "Finding temporary and specific causes for misfortune is the art of hope ... Finding permanent and universal causes for misfortune is the practice of despair." Think about a trial you are experiencing in the present. Are you finding temporary or permanent causes? Explain why?

5. Seligman's theory of the "The Explanatory Style," states that people respond to situations from either a "yes" point of view or a "no" point of view. Our "explanatory style" is how we explain things to ourselves. Which explanatory style would you say you operate from?

Read: I Peter 1:2–3 and I Peter 4:12
6. The third ingredient in the recipe of overcoming our problems is to understand that God hasn't forgotten us. He has our circumstances covered with an eternal hope. Why is it important to remind ourselves of this promise?

Group Prayer Suggestion
   Take time to pray for your group members by using the "original recipe" found in this chapter. Pray that they will have the ability to:
   1.   Discover what's important and arrange their schedules and life around eternity.

   2.   Smother the urge to live for this world only.

   3.   Understand that God has them covered—"not one is missing,

not one forgotten. God the Father has his eye on each of you ..."
(1 Peter 1:1–2 MSG).

Chapter 4:
"GOING YOUR OWN PRIDEFUL WAY"

1. Aaron Beck writes, "We all have the tendency to perceive ourselves as the lead actor of a play and to judge other people's
   behavior exclusively in reference to ourselves." How easy is it to
   view your life like this?

2. Robert writes, "The Pharisee believed ... perfection was obtainable, and the childhood question, "Are we there yet?" turned into
   a way to judge others and put them down, "I've arrived and you
   haven't." Do you believe there are Pharisees living today in the
   sense that they look down and judge others from their self-
   imposed righteous perches?

3. Below are Aaron Beck's "stages in the development of hostility."
   Have you ever traveled through this process in your anger?
   Event → Distressed → "Wronged" → Anger → Mobilize to Attack

4. Do you internalize anger or vent?

5. Robert writes, "Sometimes our situations call for gentle confrontation." Do you have a hard time confronting those who
   make you angry?

6. This week, use the formula below to help relieve some of the
   stress that produces anger:
   Confrontation minus an Emotional Charge = Alleviated Frustration.

Group Prayer Suggestion

Pray for God to give each of your small-group members a peace to confront stressful situations without an emotional charge being involved. Pray for each one to be aware of the tendency to view life from center-stage. Pray for God's view that helps us look upon our moments with eternal focus.

Chapter 5:
"WE'LL LEAVE THE LIGHT ON FOR YOU"

1. Robert writes, "Blame is a self-justifying tendency to project onto others the guilt we don't want to feel." Do you feel that other people blame you at times for their troubles?

2. Robert writes, "Escapism is running from problems instead of facing them." Can you give some examples of people you know (no names) who escape? On the graph below put an X where you see yourself in this picture.

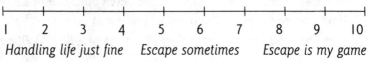

| 1 | 2 | 3 | 4 | 5 | 6 | 7 | 8 | 9 | 10 |

Handling life just fine   Escape sometimes   Escape is my game

3. Robert confessed that one of the areas where he escapes to keep from facing his own problems is into the pain of others. Discuss the reason why you think Robert escaped into the pain of others.

Read: Matthew 26:35

4. Peter denied Jesus three times but said in the beginning that he would never deny. Why do you think he succumbed to denial when he was so adamantly against it?

5. Robert writes, "Denial is the art of deceiving ourselves, so we'll

believe our own lies." It's another way to ignore our true problems. Can you list some ways people use denial?

Group Prayer Suggestion

Pray for God to give each of your small-group members the courage to get out of what Robert calls the BED—*blame, escape, denial.*

Chapter 6:
"HIGHWAYS WILL ONLY GET YOU SO FAR"

1. Whenever we open our lives up to other people, there's the risk of control. How does opening your life to other people do one of the following:
    *   *Being dominated*
    *   *Regulating your actions*
    *   *Coercing you to do things that make you feel uncomfortable*

Read: I Kings 19:21
2. Robert writes, "God will use people the way he used Elijah in Elisha's life." Have you found people who are helping you along on the journey? Describe how they help you.

Read: I Samuel 16:18–19
3. David was discovered because a servant spoke up. How are you helping others along the way? Do you have someone you are in a mentoring relationship with?

Read: Psalm 133:1
4. Robert believes community points to the larger purpose of God's Kingdom, where we say with the psalmist, "How wonderful it is, how pleasant, when brothers live together in harmony!" How are

you helping your church stay in harmony? Is harmony essential to forming community?

5. Do people have a tendency to complain more than encourage one another in church?

Group Prayer Suggestion

Take some time to pray for your mentor or pray to receive one. Pray for God to send you someone who can help you get further than your road is taking you. Also, you may want to pray for your church. Pray for community to take place in harmony.

Chapter 7:
"DETOURS, SHORTCUTS, AND ROADBLOCKS"

1. Go back and read the options on page 81 and discuss which option you think would've been better than the one Robert chose.

2. Freeman & DeWolf reference a certain scene in the movie *Blazing Saddles* where the good guys are being chased by the bad guys through the desert. The good guys have to figure out a way to slow the bad guys down. And what do they do? They set up a tollbooth. They are so focused on the *barrier* the tollbooth presents that they don't see all those miles and miles of open desert on either side of it. Have you ever been so focused on a problem that you couldn't see the miles and miles around it? On the graph below put an X where you see yourself in this picture.

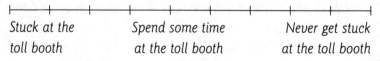

Stuck at the	Spend some time	Never get stuck
toll booth	at the toll booth	at the toll booth

3. Robert writes, "The one thing we don't have in a time of broken-ness is clarity. He believes the reason why is because we second-guess every decision. Have you found this true in your life? Why?

4. Harry Emerson Fosdick believes few people "have a chance to live their lives on the basis of their first choice. We all have to live upon the basis of our second and third choices." Do you agree with this statement? If not, why?

5. Life is too short to remain in a cycle, and the way to spot the emotional terrain of pain is by reviewing our prayers. Sometimes we pray more for release than we do for change. What is the difference between praying for release and praying for change?

6. Describe a time in your life when you've prayed more for release than change.

Group Prayer Suggestion

Take some time to pray for change. Pray for God to show you the miles and miles surrounding your problem.

Chapter 8:
"WHEN YOU FEEL LIFE SLIP-SLIDING AWAY"

1. Robert writes, "'All-or-nothing-thinking,' ... is the belief that if we don't have a perfect situation in our life at this moment, then we have nothing." Do you ever have "all-or-nothing-thinking?"

Read: Luke 12:25

2. Ernest Ligon says, "Fear must not be confused with caution." It's this dual role of fear that makes it confusing. Do you get confused about the dual role of fear?

3. Start a journal. List all of the things you're fretting about. Then wait a month and reread them to find out which ones became a reality. Appoint a time to bring this journal back to the group for discussion.

Read: 1 Samuel 17:1–31
4. David knew action confronts fear. How are you eradicating the source of your fear?

5. Charles Reynolds Brown writes, "Find yourself as one who has a definite responsibility which cannot be delegated to anybody else, and then fill your place to the brim." Do you feel that you have a purpose in life? Discuss what it means to have a purpose.

Group Prayer Suggestion
Take some time to pray for God to give you peace instead of fear. Pray for God's assurance that He's taking care of your needs. Also, pray for purpose.

Chapter 9:
"Is Life Beautiful? I Can't Ever Tell"

1. Fredrick Buechner writes, "There are lots of people who get into the habit of thinking of their time as not so much an end in itself, a time to be lived and loved and filled full for its own sake, but more as just a kind of way station on the road to somewhere else." Do you think of your time as a way station on the road to somewhere else? If so, how does that affect the present?

Read: Luke 12:27
2. Robert writes, "Jesus points out a scenic view and says, in essence, 'Stop, look, and consider. Take the scenic route for a

minute. What do you see?'" Do you spend time considering the lilies? If so, describe a scenic view that you've seen in the past. What did it reveal to you about God? Does the scenic view take time out of your schedule?

3. Thoreau noted mournfully, "The youth gets together his materials to build a bridge to the moon or perchance a palace or temple on the earth, and at length the middle-aged man concludes to build a wood-shed with them." Have you found this to be true in life? Do we lose the adventure of possibilities?

4. Have you or do you know of someone who has recently been through the "empty nest" syndrome? How can we adjust after the children marry or go off to college?

5. Robert writes about God giving a Post-it Note: "Cherish the moment." Have you ever received a Post-it Note from God? (Some call it an epiphany.)

Group Prayer Suggestion

Lift up specific prayers for those who need to slow down and catch the scenic view. Pray for those who may be experiencing the "empty nest" syndrome. Take the time this week to stop at a scenic view. At the next meeting, discuss what you experienced.

Chapter 10:
"WATCH OUT FOR BUM PIGS!"

1. If you were Robert, how would you respond to Dean's put down? Has anyone ever treated you this way? If so, discuss how it felt.

Read: 1 Peter 4:8
2. Can you love like this without becoming a doormat?

Read: Matthew 7:6
3. What did Jesus mean when he said to not throw pearls to swine? What are the pearls? Who are the swine?

Read: Genesis 21:25–30
4. Abimelech approaches Abraham with some gossip. Do you think Abimelech handled it correctly?

5. Some people are control freaks, like the grandmother in Flannery O'Connor's short story. How do you deal with them?

6. Robert writes, "A control freak weaves their lies so deep into our psyches that we can't differentiate between where we stop and the control freak begins." Can you ever be free from them?

Group Prayer Suggestion
Take time to pray for those who feel:
- *Their pearls are being trampled*
- *Swine behavior is rooting into their business*
- *Swine behavior is controlling them*

 *Chapter 11:*

"THE WORLD WILL DROWN YOU IF YOU LET IT"

1. After Robert's car fell into a sink hole, he writes, "It's easy to become the victim who says to God, "Why did you do this to me?" Have you ever been an innocent victim? How did it feel?

2. Discuss George Costanza's success at doing the "opposite." Has this ever worked for you? Is there something in your life that could benefit from an opposite view?

3. C. S. Lewis writes, "I would much rather say that every time you make a choice you are turning the central part of you, the part of you that chooses, into something a little different from what it was before. And taking your life as a whole, with all your innumerable choices, all your life long you are slowly turning this central thing either into a heavenly creature or into a hellish creature ..." How can Lewis' view change the way you think about making decisions? Does his theory make sense?

Read: Isaiah 64:8

4. The metaphors of the "clay" and the "potter" are great examples of looking at our relationship with God based on metaphors. Thinking of yourself as a metaphor, what would you say would be a good choice for you? Discuss how this relates to your relationship with God.

5. Erik Erikson, a psychologist concerned with identity, believes we learn to "win recognition by producing things." Is this true for you? If not, how do you derive your identity?

Group Prayer Suggestion

Take some time to pray for each person using the metaphor that they identified themselves with. Then for the next week, see yourself as the metaphor in everything you do.

Chapter 12:

"Suffering Along the Way"

1. Robert writes about the man who said he didn't think anyone would want to drink his cup: "And in a way the man in the red socks is right about a lot of things in life. Nobody wants to drink the cup of suffering." Discuss your view on suffering.

2. Explain your view of the codfish being chased by their natural enemy, the catfish. Does this translate to the way evil conditions our soul?

3. Can God's goodness be mistaken for suffering?

Read: Hebrews 12:7

4. Discuss the "Parable of the Milky Creek." How do you explain God's discipline?

5. Robert writes, "And God works out His purpose with His loving arm of correction and doesn't eliminate the free will of the water." Give some examples of how you think God gives mankind free will. Mark an X below in the slot that best expresses your belief.

```
├────┼────┼────┼────┼────┼────┼────┼────┤
```

God gives	*God and Man*	*Man has*
man no control	*share control*	*complete control*

Group Prayer Suggestion

Pray for God to make you loveable no matter what the circumstance.

Chapter 13:
"BOAT LAUNCHING CAN BE HAZARDOUS TO YOUR EGO"

1. Reread the story about the Olympian crew team. Is there any way to know when the unintended will outweigh the intended? Do you see this happening in your life?

Read: Judges 11:30–31; 34
2. Do you think Jephthah made a rash vow? Do you find yourself making rash decisions that could be prayed about first? It seems that Jephthah did pray, but did he pray for selfish reasons?

3. How would you answer Karen Horney's question, "What do unresolved conflicts do to our energies, our integrity, and our happiness?"

Read: 1 Kings 19:1–4
4. Robert writes, "He (Elijah) chose to live with unresolved conflict instead of facing down Jezebel's threat. He needed to settle in his spirit the sense of Divine protection." How protected by God do you feel? What could Elijah do to remedy his situation?

Read: 1 Kings 19:10
5. Elijah disqualified the positive (p. 158). Have you ever disqualified the positive?

Read: 2 Kings 7:3–11
6. Robert writes, "Every move of God takes place when we get off dead-center, when we get off this life that says I want what I want and I want it now!" How can you get off dead-center in your life to experience a fresh move of God?

Group Prayer Suggestion

Pray for God to show you unresolved conflict that may be keeping you on dead-center, and then pray for the courage to face it.

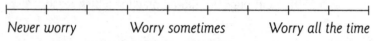

Chapter 14:
"WHEN YOU CAN ONLY SEE WHAT YOUR HEADLIGHTS REVEAL"

1. Robert writes, "We've *all* heard these voices that bring about thoughts of hopelessness." Do you battle thoughts of worry, doubt, or hopelessness? Mark an X below to indicate how often you worry.

```
|----+----+----+----+----+----+----+----|
```
Never worry   Worry sometimes   Worry all the time

Read: Jeremiah 32:1–15

2. Robert writes, "Even though it was an economical downturn in a time of war, (Jeremiah) still believed in redemption." If you were offered the same deal as Jeremiah, would you buy the land? Would you believe in redemption?

3. How does the redemption found in Jeremiah 32 relate to the redemption found in the Cross of Christ?

4. Robert writes, "Yeah," said Joseph, "He (preacher) said that if we needed anything that we should pray and ask God for it. So, last night, I prayed for a pair of shoes." Do you believe God hears prayers for shoes? Do you believe He heard Joseph's prayer?

5. Read Haddon Robinson's illustration of living by Act III (p 172). Can we really live in the light of God's final act?

6. Robert writes, "Anybody care to buy some oceanfront property in

the Christian faith." How would you answer this question? Are
Christians the only ones who can live in the light of God's
redemption?

The Word at Work . . .

What would you do if you wanted to share God's love with children on the streets of your city? That's the dilemma David C. Cook faced in 1870s Chicago. His answer was to create literature that would capture children's hearts.

Out of those humble beginnings grew a worldwide ministry that has used literature to proclaim God's love and disciple generation after generation. Cook Communications Ministries is committed to personal discipleship—to helping people of all ages learn God's Word, embrace his salvation, walk in his ways, and minister in his name.

Opportunities—and Crisis

We live in a land of plenty—including plenty of Christian literature! But what about the rest of the world? Jesus commanded, "Go and make disciples of all nations" (Matt. 28:19) and we want to obey this commandment. But how does a publishing organization "go" into all the world?

There are five times as many Christians around the world as there are in North America. Christian workers in many of these countries have no more than a New Testament, or perhaps a single shared copy of the Bible, from which to learn and teach.

We are committed to sharing what God has given us with such Christians.

A vital part of Cook Communications Ministries is our international outreach, Cook Communications Ministries International (CCMI). Your purchase of this book, and of other books and Christian-growth products from Cook, enables CCMI to provide Bibles and Christian literature to people in more than 150 languages in 65 countries.

Cook Communications Ministries is a not-for-profit, self-supporting organization. Revenues from sales of our books, Bible curricula, and other church and home products not only fund our U.S. ministry, but also fund our CCMI ministry around the world. One hundred percent of donations to CCMI go to our international literature programs.

. . . Around the World

CCMI reaches out internationally in three ways:

· Our premier International Christian Publishing Institute (ICPI) trains leaders from nationally led publishing houses around the world to develop evangelism and discipleship materials to transform lives in their countries.

· We provide literature for pastors, evangelists, and Christian workers in their national language. We provide study helps for pastors and lay leaders in many parts of the world, such as China, India, Cuba, Iran, and Vietnam.

· We reach people at risk—refugees, AIDS victims, street children, and famine victims—with God's Word. CCMI puts literature that shares the Good News into the hands of people at spiritual risk—people who might die before they hear the name of Jesus and are transformed by his love.

Word Power, God's Power

Faith Kidz, RiverOak, Honor, Life Journey, Victor, NexGen — every time you purchase a book produced by Cook Communications Ministries, you not only meet a vital personal need in your life or in the life of someone you love, but you're also a part of ministering to José in Colombia, Humberto in Chile, Gousa in India, or Lidiane in Brazil. You help make it possible for a pastor in China, a child in Peru, or a mother in West Africa to enjoy a life-changing book. And because you helped, children and adults around the world are learning God's Word and walking in his ways.

Thank you for your partnership in helping to disciple the world. May God bless you with the power of his Word in your life.

For more information about our international ministries, visit www.ccmi.org.

Additional copies of this or other Life Journey books
are available from your local Christian bookseller.

✻✻✻

If you have enjoyed this book,
or if it has had an impact on your life,
we would like to hear from you.

Please contact us at:

LIFE JOURNEY BOOKS
Cook Communications Ministries, Dept. 201
4050 Lee Vance View
Colorado Springs, CO 80918

Or visit our website: www.cookministries.com